THE PRESIDENT AND HIS POWERS

THE PRESIDENT
AND HIS POWERS

By WILLIAM HOWARD TAFT

TWENTY-SIXTH PRESIDENT OF THE UNITED STATES

WITH AN INTRODUCTION

By NICHOLAS MURRAY BUTLER

PRESIDENT OF COLUMBIA UNIVERSITY

COLUMBIA UNIVERSITY PRESS

NEW YORK AND LONDON

This book was originally published under the title *Our Chief Magistrate and His Powers*. It is based on the Columbia University Lectures, under the George Blumenthal Foundation, delivered in 1915.

INTRODUCTION

I⊤ is in no wise surprising that the continuing demand for Mr. Taft's book on the presidency should require the printing of a new edition. It is not often possible to find the duties, the opportunities and the obligations of a great public office set forth in philosophic fashion by one who has discharged those duties, enjoyed those opportunities and fulfilled those obligations.

From the more or less voluminous correspondence of Washington, of the two Adamses, of Jefferson and of Madison, one may get a fairly clear idea of the presidential office as it was in their day. The incumbency and the experience of Lincoln were of course unique, and between that time and the presidency of Roosevelt there is no elaborate written record of the personal and official activities of any president. There are, to be sure, biographies, more or less satisfactory, but of the later presidents it is only Roosevelt who, by reason of his voluminous and amazingly interesting correspondence, relates himself to the earlier presidents as one who reveals day by day the duties and activities of that great office. A president who does not write many letters and frank ones, stands little chance of being understood or appreciated by the generations that follow.

Mr. Taft's discussion is far less personal, more objective and more philosophical than any correspondence could possibly be. On that account it is more suitable to the purposes of the general reader and for those, both in the United

States and out of it, who would get a clear and exact comprehension of the functions and duties of him whom we proudly call our Chief Magistrate.

NICHOLAS MURRAY BUTLER

COLUMBIA UNIVERSITY
December 15, 1924

CONTENTS

THE PRESIDENT AND HIS POWERS

CHAPTER I

Distribution of Governmental Powers. The Veto Power

THE framers of our Constitution were much affected by Montesquieu's appreciation of the English Constitution and his insistence upon a division of the government into Legislative, Executive and Judicial branches and a separation of one from the other, as the best security for civil liberty. They, thus, made this division and separation more clearly marked and rigid than in the British Constitution. In a way that I shall attempt to describe later, there was established the power of the Judicial branch, by its decisions in litigated cases, to construe the limitations on the Executive and Legislative powers contained in the Constitution and thereby through the moral influence and force of its judgments to affect the future action of the Executive and the Congress, and restrain them within the limits of the fundamental law as declared by it. But these judgments of the Supreme Court can only be rendered in actual and litigated cases, in which one individual has sued another and in which generally some constitutional right of an individual is infringed by Legislative or Executive action. There is in the scope of the jurisdiction of both the Executive and Congress a wide field of action in which individual rights are not affected in such a way that they can be asserted and

1

vindicated in a court. In this field, the construction
of the power of each branch and its limitations must
be left to itself and the political determination of the
people who are the ultimate sovereign asserting themselves at the polls. Precedents from previous administrations and from previous Congresses create
an historical construction of the extent and limitations
of their respective powers, aided by the discussions
arising in a conflict of jurisdictions between them.
The field of action by the Executive is perhaps less
subject to judicial interpretation than that of Congress. Most legislation of doubtful validity in one
way or another ultimately comes before the Court.
And so the limitations of Congress may be much
more fully studied in the Supreme Court Reports
than those of Executive action. This makes the
definition of Executive power somewhat more difficult, and somewhat less within the usually trodden
path of students of constitutional law, than that of
Congress. By actual experience in the exercise of
Executive power, one must acquire some familiarity
with precedents not set forth in treatises and not
elaborately and carefully discussed in judicial decisions. In the necessary paucity of living ex-Presi-
dents, therefore, my empirical knowledge of the extent
and limits of our national Executive power makes
me venture to ask your attention to the subject of
these chapters.

The question of the Presidency, its duties, its responsibilities and its limitations, ought perhaps to
be settled not in the heat of the issues that constantly
arise for the decision of the incumbent, but rather in

the careful study from an unbiased standpoint of the historian and the jurist. Still no such determination will be a fair one that does not give some weight to the practical considerations that crowd upon one charged with executive responsibility. I may add, on the other hand, that retirement from office to a place of study and contemplation, rather than of action, modifies somewhat the views formed, *dum fervet opus*. This, I think, is significant of the value of having, from time to time, the constitutional limitations upon the Executive power interpreted by another branch of the government than that to whose action they apply.

The inefficient performance of their executive functions by the Continental Congress and the ad interim committee of that Congress, no one can doubt who will read the correspondence of Washington during the Revolution, or observe the stagnant chaos there was after independence was won. The example of the one-man power under George III, which he maintained by his corrupt control of Parliament, made the Convention doubtful as to the methods by which, and the persons through whom, the Executive power should be exercised. Roger Sherman, representing a minority, thought that the Executive should be the mere agent of the Legislature to carry out their will, and others thought that the Executive should not only thus be controlled, but in order to protect against abuse of powers, it should be vested in a number of persons. Randolph of Virginia is understood to have supported this view. Hamilton, at the other extreme, thought that the Executive should be single, should be elected for life, and should be given ample powers independent of the Legislative branch and absolute power to veto its enactments. The happy result which was reached between the two extremes is only one of the many instances of the triumph of clear-headed common sense, wise patriotism and the personal sacrifice of cherished notions, which we find in the compromises embodied in our wonderful Constitution.

The result in respect of the Executive, as you know, was that the President was to be elected for a term of four years, by an electoral college elected by the people of the states, or in such manner as the legislature of each state might provide, and was given wide powers, not rigidly limited, including the power of qualified veto, under which he could prevent any bill from becoming law unless it could subsequently be passed over his veto by a two-thirds vote in each House of Congress.

I am strongly inclined to the view that it would have been a wiser provision, as it was at one time voted in the Convention, to make the term of the President six or seven years, and render him ineligible thereafter. Such a change would give to the Executive greater courage and independence in the discharge of his duties. The absorbing and diverting interest in the reëlection of the incumbent, taken by those Federal civil servants who regard their own tenure as dependent upon his, would disappear and the efficiency of ad-ministration in the last eighteen months of a term would be maintained.

I think, too, it would have been better to bring the Executive a little closer in touch with Congress in the initiation of legislation and its discussion, notably in the matter of budgets and the economical adminis-tration of governmental affairs. The great problem that is forcing itself upon the attention of the American people is the method of restraining the extravagance of legislatures and of Congresses. The people them-selves are largely to blame for this, not the people as the whole, but the people divided into districts, because the constituencies of members of Congress and of Senators stimulate their representatives in a competitive effort to get as much money out of the public treasury for their respective districts as possible, and are prone to decline reëlecting representatives who fail in this contest. I have not time to dwell on the enormous burden that this selfishness of the people of each district and of their representative imposes upon the government and upon all the people. The waste of money in river and harbor bills, in public building bills, in the establishment of army posts and of navy yards at places selected, not because they are most useful to the army and navy in the economic administration of military and naval defenses, but because they are in favored districts, have had much to do with the increase by leaps and bounds of our actual governmental expenditure. Every other gov-ernment but ours has what is called a budget system. It was best developed perhaps in the English system of government, and its historical growth is interesting to trace and is useful in order to point the way to the curbing of legislative extravagance. I do not mean to say that the heads of bureaus and even the heads of departments in the Executive branch may not be prone to extravagance, but the result of my experience, which I am sure is borne out by the conclusion of others, is that the Chief Executive, because he is the one whose method of choice and whose range of duties have direct relation to the people as a whole and the government as a whole, is most likely to feel the necessity for economy in total expenditures. It is true of the governor of a state, as it is of the President of the United States. Those who are least moved by anxiety as to the totals are the members of the Legislative branch who are struggling to get as much money as they can out of the general treasury for their respective local constituencies.

In English history, the King and his Ministers ran the government, and the early struggle of Parliament was to restrain the King. The Commons of England by hard effort finally confirmed to themselves the power to refuse to the King money which he asked to carry on the government of the Kingdom. He came before them and said, "I need and request this much money to discharge the duties of the Crown," and the Commons scrutinized his demands, and frequently in the giving exacted from him conditions and limitations. More than two centuries ago, in the government that thus grew up, there was adopted a rule in Parliament that no member could be heard to move for an increase in the supplies and none would be granted unless asked by the Crown. In other words, the Crown was asking the Commons for money, and the function of the Commons was to examine the merit of the request and to cut down from the supplies asked, without power to increase them. The due course at the present day is for the Crown through its Ministers and Parliament to submit for discussion the supplies that each department of the government needs, to have such supplies voted by Parliament, without any increase. After the supplies have been voted, it becomes the duty of the Ministers of the Crown to propose to Parliament through the Chancellor of the Exchequer the budget, that is, a statement of the total proposed expenditure and of the means by which the revenue is to be raised with which to meet the cost. In this way the extravagance on the part of Parliament is avoided, and the government takes over the responsibility for economy and efficiency in government. Of course Parliament has the general legislative power, and it may pass laws imposing upon the Crown new duties of administration requiring the appropriation of additional funds to discharge these new duties. The Crown must submit an estimate for this increase. I have been perhaps more detailed in this statement than I ought to have been in this connection, for the reason that your late Constitutional Convention has grappled with the question and attempted to solve it in the proposed amendments to your Constitution upon this head. It is one of the most important steps of progress that has been taken in constitutional law in this country. In all the wild fads and nostrums that we find set forth in recent constitutional amendments adopted in various states, this stands out as a shining light of hope and a vindication of optimism. If New York succeeds in adopting this system, by which the governor submits estimates and a budget of expenditures and proposed revenues, and the legislature of New York is forbidden to increase the estimates by him submitted, the alarming expenditure and extravagance of government expenses will be halted, and this without in any degree reducing the proper legislative control of the general scope and extent of governmental action and expenditure. Upon the governor and those associated with him will be placed the responsibility for running that government which the legislature has provided by law, as efficiently and economically as it can be done, and the inconsiderate selfishness of local constituencies will be defeated. Success of this system in New York will, I doubt not, lead to a similar reform in the government at Washington. Now not only is Congress unlimited in its extravagance, due to the selfishness of the different congressional constituencies, but Congress as a whole and each House as a unit have by committee government deliberately parted with any actual efficient control of the total annual expenditures from the public treasury. Nor has Congress earnestly coöperated in the past with the Executive in efforts to secure a more economical organization of the government and the elimination of duplication of functions and greater saving and efficiency in the departments. I think, therefore, that our Federal Constitution might be improved in imposing the duty of framing a budget on the Executive and limiting the power of Congress in the voting of appropriations, so that it may give all that the Executive asks to run the government as organized by Congress through general laws, and may not have the specific power to increase the appropriations which the Executive says on his oath and his responsibility are enough to carry on the government duly established by Congress.

As every President has to do, I made many addresses, and the gentleman who introduced me, by way of exalting the occasion rather than the guest, not infrequently said that he was about to introduce one who exercised greater governmental power than any monarch in Europe. I need hardly point out the inaccuracies of this remark, by comparing the powers of the President of the United States with those of the rulers of countries in which there is not real popular legislative control. The powers of the German Emperor, of the Emperor of Austria, and the Emperor of Russia are far wider than those of the President of the United States, although there are in each of those countries legislative bodies with members more or less representative of the people, with some power of governmental control. On the other hand, in really parliamentary governments, the head of the state is less powerful than our President. In England, as it is, the King reigns, but does not govern, and the same thing is true in the Dominion of Canada, of the Governor-General. In France, the President presides, but does not govern. In such parliamentary governments, however, there is a real ruler who exercises in some important respects a greater power than the President of the United States. He is the leader of the majority in the popular house and remains in office only as long as he has that majority behind him. He is the premier, and exercises both executive and legislative functions. The executive head of the state, whether King or President or Governor-General, follows his recommendation in executive work, and he with his colleagues in the Cabinet, as responsible Ministers so-called, controls the legislation.

It would be idle to discuss which is the better form of government. It may be generally said that those who have a parliamentary or responsible government, as it is called, like that form, and that we like our form. Ours is more rigid, in that it divides the Executive from the Legislative, but is like parliamentary government in that in both the Judicial branch is independent of the other two. It is often said that parliamentary government is more responsive to the will of the people than ours in which we have the rigid system of an election of the President every four years and of a Congress every two years; whereas whenever public opinion changes in a parliamentary or responsible form of government, the government changes accordingly. This is hardly accurate. The parliamentary government is responsive to the views of the majority of the members of the more popular house, and if those views do not change, and that majority continues to support the existing Ministers of the Crown who have been selected from its members, the government will last as long as the law permits it to last. Until recently the period was seven years in England and is now five years. This majority in the popular house, the House of Commons, is always elected in a bitter political controversy and the members of the majority are always elected as political partisans. They and not the people must change their views if the political character of the government is to change.

It is true, that when a government in England gets

its power from a majority in the House of Commons, made up not of all the members of one party, but of the members of one party, united with those of smaller groups of members representing a class or special interest, then changes in the parliamentary management are likely to be more frequent. In the present Parliament, there is the Liberal Party, the Irish Party and the Labor Party. The two latter are groups, small in number as compared with the Liberal Party, but needed in making up the Ministers' majority. This gives the groups holding the balance of power an opportunity to force measures in their special interest, that as separate issues might not be approved by a majority of Parliament or of the voters of the Kingdom, a condition which is not conducive to the best considered legislation.

It is true that a parliamentary government offers an opportunity for greater effectiveness in that the same mind or minds control the executive and the legislative action, and the one can be closely suited to the other; whereas our President has no initiative in respect to legislation given him by law except that of mere recommendation, and no method of entering into the argument and discussion of the proposed legislation while pending in Congress, except that of a formal message or address. To one charged with the responsibilities of the President, especially where he has party pledges to perform, this seems a defect, but whatever I thought while in office, I am inclined now to think that the defect is more theoretical than actual. It usually happens that the party which is successful in electing a President is also successful in electing a Congress to sustain him. The natural party cohesion and loyalty, and a certain power and prestige which the President has when he enters office, make his first Congress one in which he can exercise much influence in the framing and passage of legislation to fulfil party promises. The history of the present administration and that of many administrations bear me out in this. But it is said that not infrequently the second Congress of an administration contains a majority politically adverse to the President in either one or both of its Houses which makes affirmative legislation impossible and limits congressional action to appropriation bills and non-political measures, if there are any such. The President in such a case naturally chafes under his inability to put through important bills, which he deems of the highest value. On the whole, however, I do not think the country suffers from this in an age and generation when the bane of political methods, and the danger to the best interests of the country, is in the overwhelming mass of ill-digested legislation. We live in a stage of politics, where legislators seem to regard the passage of laws as much more important than the results of their enforcement. The value of the legislation seems not to be in the good of its operation, but in its vote-getting quality, and its use as molasses for the catching of political flies. Therefore, a system in which we may have an enforced rest from legislation for two years is not bad. It affords an opportunity for proper digestion of recent legislation and for the detection of its defects.

Real progress in government must be by slow stages. Radical and revolutionary changes, arbitrarily put into operation, are not likely to be permanent or to accomplish the good which is prophesied of them. My observation of new reform legislation of a meritorious character is that Congress and its members must be educated up to its value by those who have studied it and become convinced of its wisdom. It will be found that much of the good legislation that has gone on to the statute book has been pending before successive sessions of Congress and successive Congresses until Congress and the public have become familiar with the reasons for its adoption, until discussions lasting over from one Congress to another have subjected the proposals to useful scrutiny and amendment, and until it thus acquires a form that Congress is willing to adopt. Sessions therefore at which legislation is not finally adopted, in which there is much discussion of proposed legislation, may often be most useful to the public, both in defeating legislation which ought not to be enacted and in framing for future adoption legislation which will be useful. The provision in some legislatures, Massachusetts especially, that every bill which is introduced must be considered or defeated or passed is not in my judgment a useful provision. It is apt to give unripe laws by forcing undigested and premature expression of opinion in the votes of legislators. Bars in music are used in the maintenance of harmony, and contribute to the comfort of the auditor. The world is not going to be saved by legislation, and is really benefited by an occasional two years of respite from the panacea and magic that many modern schools of politicians seem to think are to be found in the words, "Be it enacted."

The President has both legislative and executive power. Among his executive functions we shall find those which are purely executive and those which are quasi-legislative and are quasi-judicial.

The character of the veto power is purely legislative. The Constitution provides that after both Houses shall have passed a bill, it shall be presented to the President; that if he approve it, he shall sign it, but, if not, that he shall return it, with his objection, to the House in which it originated, which shall proceed to reconsider it; and that if two-thirds of the House agree to pass the bill, it shall be sent with the objections of the President to the other House, where it shall be reconsidered, and if approved by two-thirds of that House, it shall become a law.

It has been suggested by some that the veto power is executive. I do not quite see how. Of course the President has no power to introduce a bill into either House. He has the power of recommending such measures as he shall judge necessary and expedient to the consideration of Congress. But he takes no part in the running discussion of the bill after it is introduced or in its amendments. He has no power to veto parts of the bill and allow the rest to become a law. He must accept it or reject it, and his rejection of it is not final unless he can find one more than one-third of one of the Houses to sustain him in his veto. But even with these qualifications, he is still a participant in the legislation. Except for his natural and proper anxiety not to oppose the will of the two great legislative bodies, and to have harmony in the government, the reasons which control his action must be much like those which affect the action of the members of Congress.

A discussion of the veto power by Mr. Edward Campbell Mason, in a Harvard publication, gives an interesting view of its origin. The author expresses the opinion that the veto is the result of the shrinking of what was once a broad affirmative legislative function of the King. He says that in early days laws were enacted on a petition of Parliament to the King, asking for legislation, and that the law became effective by the King's proclamation declaring the law as he wished it to be. For a long period the King did not confine himself to the request of Parliament in their petition; but on the occasion of each request through his proclamation exercised the affirmative power of formulating laws. As Parliament acquired greater influence they resented the King's proclaiming something different from that which they requested. They therefore presented to the King the proposed statute drawn in proper and exact terms and successfully resisted his giving it new form and substance. He was thereafter required to proclaim the legislation as requested or veto it. His function in legislation thus became one of negation only. It has been contended that the President may not exercise the veto power except when the bill presented to him is unconstitutional. Such a view of his duty is supposed to find color of support in a proposal made and strongly advocated in the Constitutional Convention. It provided for the revision of bills which had passed both Houses by a Council, to include the President and the Supreme Judges, with the power to reject bills which had passed both Houses when they transgressed the constitutional limits of Congressional discretion. It cannot be said, however, that the provision for the Executive veto as adopted in the Constitution implies any such limitation. It is true that the power is one of negation only, but the history of its origin shows that even in its qualified form, it is legislative in its nature, a brake rather than a steam chest, but nevertheless a very important part of the machinery for making laws. The Constitution makes the President's veto turn on the question whether he approves the bill or not. The term "approve" is much too broad to be given the narrow construction by which it shall only authorize the President to withhold his signature when the reason for his disapproval of the bill is its invalidity. No better word could be found in the language to embrace the idea of passing on the merits of the bill. If anything has been established by actual precedents, it is that a President in signing or withholding signature, must consider the wisdom of the bill as one of those responsible for its character and effect. Mr. Mason says there were only four Presidents who did not veto bills on their merits. They were Washington, the Adamses and Jefferson. All the others have done so, and as to the four named, it is possible that through the agency of friendly Congresses they were able to kill bills without resorting to the veto. There are other ways of killing a cat than by choking it with butter. It is often a good deal easier for the President to prevent the passage of a bill by conference with friendly committees. It does not "rock the boat" so much.

Of course vetoes are more frequent when the President and Congress differ politically. They were very frequent in Mr. Johnson's administration when there was bitterly opposed to him a two-thirds majority of Republicans in each House. Again in the time of Mr. Hayes, the lower House of Congress was Democratic during his whole four years. Both Houses were Democratic in his last two years. This led to a number of vetoes by Mr. Hayes of bills enacted to paralyze the enforcement of Congressional election laws, and also of measures concerning the exclusion of Chinese, and the monetary policy of the United States. In Mr. Cleveland's first term, he had an adverse Congress, which resulted in many vetoes of special pension bills. President Grant, President Harrison and I had to face politically hostile Congresses, which naturally led to an expressed difference of opinion between the Executive and Congress as to the wisdom of proposed legislation. It is at such a time that one hears from the opposition Congressmen eloquent and emphatic denunciation of "the exercise of royal prerogative by the incumbent of the White House to defeat the will of the people." When one new in the Presidential office first hears a philippic of this kind, visions of the fate of Charles I may trouble him somewhat, but after a time, especially if he has indulged the habit of reading past Congressional Records, he becomes accustomed to the well-worn expressions of legislators whom the veto of a favorite bill has disappointed. There is a well-known aphorism that men are different, but husbands are all alike. The same idea may be paraphrased with respect to Con-

gressmen. Congressmen are different, but when in
opposition to an administration they are very much
alike in their attitude and in their speeches. In look-
ing back through the Congressional debates, and in
attempting to run down the history of the improvement of the White House grounds, I was much amused
to read the speech of an opposition Congressman
in the severest condemnation of the expenditure by
President Van Buren of a comparatively small sum
appropriated by Congress to improve the appearance
of the grounds of the White House by some landscape
gardening and tree planting. He said in effect that
the President was aping the royalties of Europe in
attempting to create an orangery in the rear of his
palace, in which in majestic seclusion he might stretch
his royal legs. As I read this speech, I could not but
think that the genus of opposition Congressmen had
not lost its distinctive qualities.

In the exercise of the veto power, the truth is that
it often happens that the President more truly represents the entire country than does the majority vote
of the two Houses. His constituency is the electorate
of the United States, and by reason of that he is much
freer from the influence of local prejudices and of the
play of those special territorial and state interests,
which, brought together by log-rolling methods, sometimes constitute a majority in both Houses for extrav-
agant or unwise legislation. To hold up the use of the
Presidential veto as an exercise of royal prerogative
is of course utterly absurd. It is true that the function finds its prototype in the royal veto of the British
Constitution, but no King of England has dared to

exercise it for two-hundred years. He would lose his throne if he did. Under our Constitution the veto is not the act of an hereditary monarch, but of one elected by all the people to represent all the people and charged by the fundamental law with the responsibility and duty of its exercise in proper cases.

In considering a bill presented to him for signature, it is the duty of the President of course to veto a bill no matter how much he approves its expediency, if he believes that it is contrary to the constitutional limitations upon the power of Congress. He has taken an oath to the best of his ability "to preserve, protect and defend the Constitution of the United States," and he cannot escape his obligation to do so when the question before him is whether he shall approve the bill passed by both Houses which violates the Constitution he has given his plighted faith to maintain and enforce. His duty is as high and exacting in this matter as is the duty of the Supreme Court of the United States. Indeed, his function in this regard is somewhat broader than that of the Court. The question with him is whether, in his judgment, the bill is inconsistent with the Constitution. The question which the Court has to consider when an act of Congress is before it and its validity is questioned, is not whether the Court as an original question thinks the act to be a violation of the Constitution. The fact that Congress, a coordinate branch of the government, has enacted the law, and presumably has decided it to be within its legislative power, raises a very strong presumption that the act is valid. The Court, before holding otherwise, is bound to find that beyond reasonable doubt the act is not within the limit of the discretion of the legislature in construing its own powers to decide that the act in question is within those powers. When a branch of the government is vested with a power, defined and limited, it must first construe the limitations upon its own powers in exercising them; and what the Supreme Court has to say is that it has abused that discretion and beyond a reasonable doubt has transgressed its limits. It may seem that this is not a broad distinction, but practically it may be made a real one by a conscientious court. If the Court has any doubt about the validity of a law, it is bound to sustain it, and it has no right to set aside a law merely because of a difference of opinion between it and the legislature as to the legislative powers.

This difference has been emphasized by the elder Professor Thayer of Harvard in his comments on the Constitution. He has wisely and ably explained and emphasized the necessity for maintaining the distinction. A serious doubt of the validity of a proposed bill may well lead a member of Congress to vote against it, or the President to veto it; but such a doubt would not justify the Court in treating the act as a nullity, unless it reaches an indisputable conviction that Congress has exceeded its powers, after indulging the properly strong presumption in favor of the act's validity. It may very well happen, therefore, that a President may veto a bill, Congress may pass it over his veto, the Supreme Court may sustain the law, and yet the President and the Court have the same serious doubt as to its validity which would properly lead to the

President's veto but not to the Court's annulment of it after it has been passed by Congress. I can illustrate what I say by referring to a bill which I vetoed and which was passed over my veto. It was the so-called Webb bill, which declared the shipping of liquor from one state to another, where its sale was unlawful by the law of the state, to be Federally unlawful. It seemed to me that this was in effect a delegation of power to the states to make differing rules with respect to interstate commerce in something which up to this time has been regarded as a lawful subject of such commerce. If Congress wished to declare liquor an unlawful subject of commerce from one state to another, Congress would have the power; but to attribute to Congress the power to say that one state might declare something unlawful commerce among the states, while another might declare it lawful, seemed to me to be a serious interference with the proper uniform and beneficent operation of the interstate commerce clause. I properly had much less hesitation in vetoing the bill than the Supreme Court should have in declaring it to be beyond the permissible limits of Congressional discretion. In other words, the Court may entertain the same serious doubt of the validity of the bill that led to my veto of it, and still not find the question so clear as to overcome the presumption in favor of the validity of the law because Congress has enacted it. I emphasize this point because I think it is of the highest importance that the constitutional validity of a measure should be fairly considered in the legislature and by him who exercises the veto power.

English publicists have criticized the course of discussion under a written Constitution by our legislatures. They maintain that it leads to a consideration of questions of the validity of proposed legislation rather than of its expediency. I do not think that this criticism is either weighty or correct. We do not discuss the validity of the bills in the legislatures enough. The governors of the states do not consider the constitutionality of bills presented them for signature as they ought. A measure proposed is popular with the constituents of a legislator, and if a question is raised as to its constitutional validity, he is prone to say, "Well, my people wish it. If it is invalid, the court will declare it to be invalid. Therefore, why should I run the risk of incurring unpopularity when it is not my function to enforce the Constitution?" Laws are thus passed through legislatures which palpably violate the Constitution just because constituents of legislators think that the law would be a good thing. The governor signs it with the same view. The burden is thus transferred to the Court. The Court holds the law to be invalid and the popular odium arising from a defeat of the measure is visited upon the Court, which alone of the three branches of the government has respected its oath of office in the preservation of the Constitution. This is one of the fruitful sources of the unjust attacks upon the courts of the country of which we have had so many in the last ten years. You well remember the story which Mr. Roosevelt tells of a conversation which he had with the Tammany politician, Tim Campbell, when they were both members of the legislature, in which Tim appealed to him

to vote for a particular bill of his and Mr. Roosevelt
replied, "I cannot do it, Tim, because it is plainly
unconstitutional." This called forth from Tim the
well-known expression, "What the divil is the Constitution between frinds?" That is the exact spirit
which has led to the neglect of their constitutional
obligation by legislators, and their enactment of so
many invalid measures. I have sometimes been inclined to think that after his invention and recommendation of the recall of judicial decisions, Mr. Roosevelt
was leaning a little more to Tim's view of the Constitution than at the time when this conversation was
held.

The Constitution provides that if the President does
not return the bill presented to him within ten days
(Sundays excepted) after its presentation, it is to
become law just as if he had signed it, unless Congress
by adjourning prevents its return, in which case it is
not to become a law. This enables the President, at
the close of a session, when bills are presented to him
in great number, and when he usually goes to the
Capitol for the purpose of signing them, just before
the adjournment of Congress, to defeat a bill by what
is called a pocket veto, that is by failing to sign it.
If he does not return it to Congress with his objections,
there is no opportunity for Congress to pass it over
his veto, and therefore his failure to sign is final.

It has never been decided by the Supreme Court
whether a President by signing a bill within ten days
after its passage may give it validity as a law if Congress adjourns within that ten days, and before his
signature. The Supreme Court has said that he may

sign a bill during a recess of Congress. Practice makes it clear, however, that he may not do this after adjournment. There is only one instance of such a signature. President Monroe failed to sign a bill which he had intended to sign. After conferring with his Cabinet, he decided it was wiser to ask Congress to reënact it. President Lincoln did sign a bill after an adjournment and the bill was filed with the Secretary of State and printed among the statutes. When the matter was brought to the attention of the Senate, however, the power of the President to do so was questioned and denied, and a new bill of substantially the same purport passed both Houses and was signed by the President.

The language of the Constitution with reference to what the President shall do with a bill leaves only two alternatives, one that if he approve it, he shall sign it, the other that if he does not approve it, he shall return it with his objections to Congress. It does provide that if he fails to return it within ten days, it shall become a law, but this would seem to be only a provision for his neglect. In practice, however, some Presidents have allowed bills to become law without their signature, with the idea, I presume, that their objections to the bill do not justify a veto. Mr. Cleveland looked at the matter in this way when he allowed the Gorman-Wilson Tariff bill to become a law without his signature, though he denounced it in most emphatic terms in a letter to Mr. Catchings of the House as "an act of perfidy and dishonor." My own judgment is that the wiser course in such a case is for the President to sign the bill, with a memorandum of his reasons for doing so, in spite of his objections.

The Federal Executive veto does not include the power to veto a part of a bill. The lack of such a power in the President has enabled Congress at times to bring to bear a pressure on him to permit legislation to go through that otherwise he would veto. Appropriation bills are necessary for the life of the government, and if Congress by putting what is called a "rider" of general legislation on one of these says, "We'll hamstring the government in respect to the departments that these appropriation bills support, unless you consent to this," it puts the President in an embarrassing situation.

In President Hayes' Administration, one of the issues that he had with the Democratic Congress was in respect to the enforcement of the Federal Congressional election laws. The Democratic Congress insisted first in imposing a rider on the Military Appropriation bill for the support of the army, providing that the President should not be able to use his civil officers to maintain peace at the polls. This really had no relation to the use of the army to interfere with elections. President Hayes vetoed the bill. Congress finally passed the Army Appropriation bill without the rider, but thereupon passed the Legislative, Executive and Judicial Appropriation bill, with a similar rider, which the President again vetoed. Then Congress passed this latter appropriation bill, but in order to prevent the use of marshals to preserve peace at the polls, left out any provision for the marshals and the executive officers of the courts of the United States. That state of affairs continued for two years, to the great embarrassment of the courts.

Finally, Congress surrendered after the election of President Garfield, and paid the salaries, fees and expenses of the marshals and of the executive officers of the courts which had been withheld from them for two years. In the course of the controversy, President Hayes used this language :

The enactment of this bill into a law will establish a precedent which will tend to destroy the equal independence of the several branches of the Government. Its principle places not merely the Senate and the Executive, but the Judiciary also, under the coercive dictation of the House. The House alone will be the judge of what constitutes a grievance, and also of the means and measure of redress. An act of Congress to protect elections is now the grievance complained of ; but the House may on the same principle determine that any other act of Congress, a treaty made by the President with the advice and consent of the Senate, a nomination or appointment to office, or that a decision or opinion of the Supreme Court is a grievance, and that the measure of redress is to withhold the appropriations required for the support of the offending branch of the Government.

Believing that this bill is a dangerous violation of the spirit and meaning of the Constitution, I am compelled to return it to the House in which it originated without my approval. The qualified negative with which the Constitution invests the President is a trust that involves a duty which he can not decline to perform. With a firm and conscientious purpose to do what I can to preserve unimpaired the constitutional powers and equal independence, not merely of the Executive, but of every branch of the Government, which will be imperiled by the adoption of the principle of this bill, I desire earnestly to urge upon the House of Representatives a return to the wise and wholesome usage of the early days of the Republic, which excluded from appropriation bills all irrelevant legislation.

Congress attempted the same method in my own administration, when a rider was placed upon the great Sundry Civil Appropriation bill forbidding the use of a special appropriation to enforce the anti-trust law act in prosecuting farmers and trades-unions who were found violating that act. This introduced, it seemed to me, a most pernicious discrimination and was calculated and intended to produce a lack of uniformity in the application of what should be a general law. It created a privileged class and was insisted on merely for political purposes. I vetoed the bill. A similar bill with a similar rider was subsequently signed by President Wilson, but under protest against the principle of such discrimination.

It has been suggested that such an abuse of power by Congress, for that it certainly is, could be avoided by giving to the President the power to veto special items and clauses of an appropriation bill. This power is exercised by some governors in states, notably the governor of New York. While for some purposes, it would be useful for the Executive to have the power of partial veto, if we could always be sure of its wise and conscientious exercise, I am not entirely sure that it would be a safe provision. It would greatly enlarge the influence of the President, already large enough from patronage and party loyalty and other causes. I am inclined to think that it is better to trust to the action of the people in condemning the party which becomes responsible for such riders, than to give, in such a powerful instrument like this, a temptation to its sinister use by a President eager for continued political success. This use by Congress of riders upon appropriation bills to force a President to consent to legislation which he disapproves shows a spirit of destructive factionalism and a lack of a sense of responsibility for the maintenance of the government. If such a sense of responsibility does not pervade all branches of the government, Executive, Legislative and Judicial, the government cannot remain a going concern. Instances of abuses of this sort by Congress, therefore, must be regarded as exceptional, as indeed they are, and an effort to remedy them by a change in constitutional provision would be legislation intended to pump patriotism into public officers by force. This method will certainly be found futile if such patriotism and sense of responsibility do not exist without it. If it is urged that the President should have the power to veto items in an appropriation bill to restrain Legislative extravagance, the answer is that this is not the best way. The proper remedy for that evil is the budget amendment proposed by the Constitutional Convention of New York, which I have already discussed.

CHAPTER II

THE MINOR POWERS OF THE PRESIDENT

In the first chapter, I considered the general distribution of governmental powers and the veto power of the President, his only Legislative function. I now begin a consideration of his Executive functions, in some of which he or his subordinates exercise what I shall hope to show are quasi-legislative and quasi-judicial powers. In this chapter, I propose to discuss what may perhaps be called the minor functions of the President, and shall devote some of the time also to the personal aspects of the great office. I class among the President's minor functions, the powers to consult the heads of Executive departments as to the questions arising in their respective departments, to inform Congress of the state of the Union, to recommend measures to it which he may deem wise, expedient and necessary; to issue commissions to officers of the United States, and to convene Congress in extra session, and adjourn it in case of disagreement between the Houses.

The Constitution does not use the term "Cabinet," and does not recognize a Presidential Council as a legal body. There has crept into some statutes, loosely drawn, the phrase "Cabinet Officer," and the Supreme Court Judges in their discussions of cases sometimes use it. It will be observed, however, that while the Constitution refers to the head of a department and authorizes the President to make him an adviser as to matters in his own department, it contains no suggestion of a meeting of all the department heads, in consultation over general governmental matters. The Cabinet is a mere creation of the President's will. It is an extra-statutory and extra-constitutional body. It exists only by custom. If the President desired to dispense with it, he could do so. As it is, the custom is for the Cabinet to meet twice a week, and for the President to submit to its members questions upon which he thinks he needs their advice, and for the members to bring up such matters in their respective departments as they deem appropriate for Cabinet conference and general discussion.

In the British government, the Cabinet is not a statutory body. It exists there, as with us, only by custom. But this fact does not derogate from the permanence and importance of the English Cabinet, because, unlike ours, the constitution of government in Great Britain is largely by custom. The distinctive feature in the present British political structure is that a vote in the House of Commons, indicating a want of confidence in the Premier and his associates, requires their resignation; yet this only abides in custom. The English Premier in selecting his associates in his Cabinet takes those members of Parliament who will effectively coöperate with him in retaining the indispensable backing of the House of Commons majority. It is needful for a ministry, therefore, that the members of the Cabinet in such a government shall be of independent strength and influence with parliamentary members. They are partners of the Premier and not merely his appointees and advisers, and have an importance which Cabinet officers do not have with us. As a member of the government, each English Cabinet officer must be prepared on the floor of one House or the other to answer questions, defend the government, and advocate the legislation which the government urges, and for which it becomes responsible. It follows that an English Cabinet officer must have qualifications not now required of a member of a Presidential Cabinet.

I am strongly in favor of a change in our existing system, by which the importance and influence of Cabinet officers shall be increased. Without any change in the Constitution, Congress might well provide that heads of departments, members of the President's Cabinet, should be given access to the floor of each House to introduce measures, to advocate their passage, to answer questions, and to enter into the debate as if they were members, without of course the right to vote. Without any express constitutional authority, Congress has done this in the case of delegates from the territories. Why may it not therefore do it with respect to the heads of departments?

This would impose on the President greater difficulty in selecting his Cabinet, and would lead him to prefer men of legislative experience who have shown their power to take care of themselves in legislative debate. It would stimulate the head of each department by the fear of public and direct inquiry into a more thorough familiarity with the actual operations of his department and into a closer supervision of its business. On the other hand, it would give the President what he ought to have, some direct initiative in legislation and an opportunity through the presence of his competent representatives in Congress to keep each House advised of the facts in the actual operation of the government. The time lost in Congress over useless discussion of issues that might be disposed of by a single statement from the head of a department, no one can appreciate unless he has filled such a place. In my annual message, December 19, 1912, I urged this proposal upon Congress, as follows :

This is not a new proposition. In the House of Representatives, in the Thirty-eighth Congress, the proposition was referred to a select committee of seven Members. The committee made an extensive report, and urged the adoption of the reform. The report showed that our history had not been without illustration of the necessity and the examples of the practice by pointing out that in early days Secretaries were repeatedly called to the presence of either House for consultation, advice, and information. It also referred to remarks of Mr. Justice Story in his Commentaries on the Constitution, in which he urgently presented the wisdom of such a change. This report is to be found in Volume I of the Reports of Committees of the First Session of the Thirty-eighth Congress, April 6, 1864.

Again, on February 4, 1881, a select Committee of the Senate recommended the passage of a similar bill, and made a report in which, while approving the separation of the three branches, the executive, legislative, and judicial, they point out as reason for the proposed change that, although having a separate existence, the branches are "to coöperate, each with the other, as the different members of the human body must coöperate, with each other, in order to form the figure and perform the duties of a perfect man.

The report is as follows :

This system will require the selection of the strongest men to be heads of departments and will require them to be well equipped with the knowledge of their offices. It will also require the strongest men to be the leaders of Congress and participate in debate. It will bring these strong men in contact, perhaps into conflict, to advance the public weal, and thus stimulate their abilities and their efforts, and will thus assuredly result to the good of the country.

If it should appear by actual experience that the heads of departments in fact have not time to perform the additional duty imposed on them by this bill, the force of their offices should be increased or the duties devolving on them personally should be diminished. An under-secretary should be appointed to whom could be confided that routine of administration which requires only order and accuracy. The principal officers could then confine their attention to those duties which require wise discretion and intellectual activity. Thus they would have abundance of time for their duties under this bill. Indeed, your committee believes that the public interest would be subserved if the Secretaries were relieved of the harassing cares of distributing clerkships and closely supervising the mere machinery of the departments. Your committee believes that the adoption of this bill and the effective execution of its provisions will be the first step toward a sound civil-service reform which will secure a larger wisdom in the adoption of policies and a better system in their execution.

(Signed)

GEO. H. PENDLETON.
W. B. ALLISON.
D. W. VOORHEES.
J. G. BLAINE.
M. C. BUTLER.
JOHN J. INGALLS.
O. H. PLATT.
J. T. FARLEY.

It would be difficult to mention the names of higher authority in the practical knowledge of our government than those which are appended to this report.

Official minutes are not kept of the Cabinet meetings. Everything is informal, except that the President sits at the head of the table, and the seats of the Cabinet members are assigned around the table according to official precedence, that is according to the order in which under the law the Cabinet officers succeed to the Presidency on the death of the President and the Vice-President, which is nearly in accordance with the order of the establishment of the various departments.

The Executive office of the President is not a recording office. The vast amount of correspondence that goes through it, signed either by the President or his Secretaries, does not become the property or a record of the government, unless it goes on to the official files of the department to which it may be addressed. The retiring President takes with him all of the correspondence, original and copies, which he carried on during his administration. Thus there is lost to public record some of the most interesting documents of governmental origin bearing on the history of an administration. It is a little like what Mr. Charles Francis Adams told me of the diplomatic records of the British Foreign Office. It has long been the custom for the important Ambassadors of Great Britain to carry on a personal correspondence with the Secretary of State for Foreign Affairs, which is not put upon the files of the department, but which gives a much more accurate and detailed account of the diplomatic relations of Great Britain than the official files. The only way in which historians can get at this, is through the good offices of the families of the deceased Ambassadors and Foreign Secretaries in whose private files they may be preserved.

Originally the State Department was supposed to be the department through which Executive acts were made public, and in which they were recorded. The Secretary of State is the custodian of the great seal of the government, and now when the President acts in general matters not affecting a particular department, and his act needs attestation by seal, the Secretary of State witnesses the signature of the President and attaches the seal. In departmental matters, however, where the President has to act, as in issuing commissions for officers in particular departments, the commissions are signed by the President, attested by the Secretary of the particular department, and a seal of that department attached. Thus the commissions of Federal Judges bear the signatures of the President and the Attorney-General, those of army officers the signatures of the President and the Secretary of War, and those of naval officers the signatures of the President and the Secretary of the Navy.

Referring again to the Cabinet meetings, Mr. Lincoln is said to have remarked that in the Cabinet after discussion and intimation of opinions, there was only one vote — and that unanimous — it was the vote of the President. It is interesting and instructive to note Mr. Jefferson's comment on the operation of the Cabinet in Washington's day. A French publicist wrote him a letter advocating a plural executive for a free government, and asked his comment upon it. He answered, dissenting from the publicist's view, and approving the plan of our Constitution as follows:

The failure of the French Directory seems to have authorized a belief that the form of a plurality, however promising in theory, is impracticable with men constituted with the ordinary passions, while the tranquil and steady tenor of our single executive, during a course of twenty-two years of the most tempestuous times the history of the world has ever presented, gives a rational hope that this important problem is at length solved. Aided by the counsels of a Cabinet of heads of departments originally four, but now five, with whom the President consults, either singly or all together, he has the benefit of their wisdom and information, brings their views to one center, and produces an unity of action and direction in all the branches of the government. The excellence of this construction of the executive power has already manifested itself here under very opposite circumstances. During the administration of our first President, his Cabinet of four members were equally divided by as marked an opposition of principle as monarchism and republicanism could bring into conflict. Had that Cabinet been a directory, like positive and negative quantities in algebra, the opposing wills would have balanced each other and produced a state of absolute inaction. But the President heard with calmness the opinions and reasons of each, decided the course to be pursued, and kept the government steadily in it, unaffected by the agitation. The public knew well the dissensions of the Cabinet, but never had an uneasy thought on their account, because they knew also they had provided a regulating power which would keep the machine in steady movement.

The picture of the Cabinet of Washington's day, with Jefferson sitting on one side of the table and Hamilton on the other, at sword's point on most political and governmental issues, is very interesting. The admirable poise of the Father of his Country was never more clearly proven than by the fact that he was able to carry on an administration as long as he did, with such a division in his Cabinet. All Cabinets are not like this. Many of them are most harmonious, and to many of the participants such meetings bring back the pleasantest memories. Mr. Jefferson himself, in commenting on his own Cabinet, gives a very different picture from that of the Cabinet of Washington, for he says of his own Cabinet to the same correspondent, in the letter I have already referred to :

There never arose, during the whole time, an instance of an unpleasant thought or word between the members. We sometimes met under differences of opinion, but scarcely ever failed, by conversing and reasoning, so to modify each other's ideas as to produce an unanimous result. Yet, able and amicable as the members were, I am not certain this would have been the case, had each possessed equal and independent powers. Ill-defined limits of their respective departments, jealousies, trifling at first, but nourished and strengthened by repetition of occasions, intrigues without doors of designing persons to build an importance to themselves on the divisions of others, might, from small beginnings, have produced persevering oppositions. But the power of decision in the President left no object for internal dissension, and external intrigue was stifled in embryo by the knowledge which incendiaries possessed, that no division they could foment, would change the course of the executive power.

It is noteworthy that the Cabinet in which there was more of rivalry and intrigue and bitterness than in any, except that of Washington, was Lincoln's. Thus the division of their Cabinets into cliques, the disloyalty of some of them and their conflicting ambitions greatly increased the heavy burdens of our two greatest Presidents.

The power and duty of the President to inform Congress on the state of the Union, and to recommend measures for its adoption, need very little comment, except to say that President Washington and President Adams treated the discharge of this duty as the occasion for visiting Congress in person and delivering their communications orally. The Senate in Washington's day was a small body of twenty-eight or thirty, and when the President had made a treaty, or was about to make one, and wished advice and consent of the Senate, he repaired in person to the Senate Chamber. President Washington had one annoying experience, of which Senator Maclay speaks in his diary: Through the assistance of General Knox, Secretary of War, who had dealt much with the Indians, he had made treaties with certain tribes. He went with the treaties to the Senate to ask its consent, and Knox accompanied him. Washington explained the treaties and asked their confirmation. The Senate wished to delay and put the matter over. Maclay says that he made the motion to postpone because he saw no chance of a fair investigation of a subject while the President sat there with his Secretary of War, to support his opinions and overawe the timid and neutral part of the Senate. It was suggested that the matter be referred to a committee. "As I sat down," Maclay says, "the President of the United States started up in a violent fret. 'This defeats every purpose of my coming here,' were the first words that he said. He then went on that he had brought his Secretary of War with him to give every necessary information; that the Secretary of War knew all about the business, and yet he was delayed and could not go on with the matter. However, he said he did not object to postponement until a later day." Maclay continues: "We waited for him to withdraw. He did so with a discontented air. Had he been any other man than the man whom I wish to regard as the first character in the world, I would have said, with sullen dignity. On the day appointed, the President came again, and then there was a great discussion in his presence, and a tedious discussion."

My impression is that Washington succeeded in securing the confirmation of the treaties, although Maclay does not make it clear. Another account of this, from a different source, and perhaps untrustworthy, says that Washington was heard by one who was near to utter an oath to Knox as he left the Senate. I am not in favor of profanity and do not wish to uphold it even in so eminent a person as the Father of our Country, but I had such a similar experience in attempting to secure the advice and consent of the Senate to my General Arbitration Treaties, which another Knox presented to them, that I confess to having a warm fellow feeling for President Washington in this unlovely expression, if he uttered it. I have read much of George Washington and have always had the profoundest admiration for the qualities which he had in such a high degree, of poise, courage, self-restraint and judgment, which without the brilliant intellectual faculties and acquirements of his contemporaries, enabled him to influence and control them all by inspiring in them a profound respect for his sense of justice, his disinterested patriotism, his high ideals, his personal force and courage and his common sense. It is difficult to get close to him as a man, however, or to feel in reading of him that personal affection that is constantly being stimulated in reminiscences of Lincoln. Such an incident as this I have related, however, of Washington shows the human side of him as a man of good red blood and makes me, because of my personal experience, come closer to him than ever before.

Jefferson had no pleasure or facility in public speaking. When he came into the office of President, therefore, he preferred to send to Congress written messages, and his practice was so formidable a precedent that this has been the custom of the Presidents down to the present administration, when President Wilson has introduced again the old practice of a personal address to both Houses. I think the change is a good one. Oral addresses fix the attention of the country on Congress more than written communications, and by fixing the attention of the country on Congress, they fix the attention of Congress on the recommendations of the President. I cannot refrain from a smile, however, when I think of the Democratic oratory which was lost because Mr. Roosevelt or I did not inaugurate such a change. The eloquent sentences that would have resounded from the lips of Senator Ollie James or Senator John Sharp Williams, those faithful followers of Jefferson, in denunciation of the introduction of "such a royal ceremony in a speech from the Throne," I could supply with little effort of the imagination. Surely a member of the Jeffersonian Party has some advantages in the Presidential chair.

It is the constitutional duty of the President to issue commissions to all officers of the United States. This, I think, is the greatest manual duty the President has to perform. When you consider all the officers in the government who are entitled to commissions, and in addition to this, the number of letters in the President's correspondence, you can understand that a substantial part of each business day is occupied with signatures. Of course the shorter the President's name, the easier his work. As I was able to sign with only seven letters, I had an advantage over my predecessor and my successor. In Washington's day, and later, all the letters patent for land and inventions had to be signed by the President, but fortunately for his more recent successors, Congress has authorized the President to designate some one else to perform this duty. I do not suppose Congress could relieve him of the burden of signing commissions, in view of the mandatory language of the Constitution.

The question of commissions seems a simple and formal one, and yet out of it came one of the greatest cases that was ever decided in this country, a case that had more direct bearing on the organic structure of this government than any in the history of the great cases decided by the Supreme Court. I refer to the case of Marbury *vs.* Madison. That case was not only of capital importance from a governmental standpoint, but it was part of the interesting personal and political history of the struggle of two giants among our statesmen and jurists. Thomas Jefferson was not in the convention that framed the Constitution. He was induced to refrain from open opposition to its ratification on a promise that a bill of rights would be added to it by amendment. In his view of government he took the democratic extreme. He was profoundly suspicious of the monarchical tendencies of the Federalist group, especially of Hamilton. As soon as the Constitution was adopted, two parties formed themselves, the Republicans and the Federalists, with Jefferson at the head of one and Hamilton at the head of the other. The Federalist Party remained in power under Washington and Adams, and then in the election of 1801, Adams was defeated by Jefferson. John Marshall, who had been a young man during the Revolution and a private soldier in the Continental Army, had taken part in the ratification of the Constitution in the Virginia Constitutional Convention, was a Federalist member of Congress in Adams' administration, and became Adams' last Secretary of State. After Adams was defeated and before Jefferson was elected and took his seat, Adams appointed Marshall to be Chief Justice, and he was confirmed in the interval by a Federalist majority in the Senate. When the Federalists saw they were going out of power, they took advantage of the fact that they controlled the Presidency and the Congress in the interval between the election and the succession of the new administration, and passed a law creating a new Circuit Court which was to be an intermediate court between the District Court and the Supreme Court, and provision was made for the appointment of sixteen judges. President Adams appointed these judges and most of them were Federalists. They were confirmed upon the night of March 3d, preceding the 4th of March when Jefferson was to take his oath. They were known as the Midnight Judges. This action by a defeated party roused the indignation of Jefferson and the Republicans. Madison, whom Jefferson designated to act as Secretary of State, was very prompt and insistent, so tradition has it, in taking over from Marshall, who continued to act as Secretary till the close of Adams' term, the Department of State. It is said that Marshall in commenting on Madison's urgency felicitated himself that he got away from the office with his own hat. The Republican Party was determined to abolish the Midnight

Judges, and they promptly passed a law for this purpose. When the law was on its passage, it was argued by the Federalists that it was unconstitutional because United States Judges must hold their offices for life. Fearing that John Marshall, who had then taken his seat as Chief Justice, and his Federalist colleagues in the Supreme Court might reach this conclusion, Congress postponed the time for the meeting of the Court for more than a year. When the Court met, no effort was made to test the validity of the repeal of the Circuit Court Act, but a cause was presented involving an issue quite as personal to Jefferson and Madison. Adams had appointed one Marbury to be Justice of the Peace in the District of Columbia for five years. The Senate confirmed him. Adams signed the Commission and. sent it to Marshall as Secretary of State, who signed it and attached the seal. By some oversight, it was not delivered to the appointee, and Adams and Marshall went out of office. Marbury thereupon applied to Madison for it, and Madison declined to deliver it. Marbury filed a petition in the Supreme Court of the United States for a mandamus to compel Madison to deliver him the Commission. An Act of Congress authorized a proceeding in mandamus in the Supreme Court, but the restrictions upon the jurisdiction of the Court in the Constitution forbade it. For the first time there was flatly presented the question whether the Supreme Court was bound to take an act of Congress duly passed by that body as conclusively valid, or, if the Court found the act to be in violation of the Constitution, it could hold the law invalid and proceed as if the law had never been passed.   This was the great issue in the case, and it is this which constitutes its transcendent importance.

The Chief Justice, speaking for the Court, held that in any case coming before it in which the rights of the parties were affected by what purported to be a statute of Congress, the Court could not avoid deciding whether it was the law or not; that when there was an inevitable inconsistency between the statutory law and the fundamental law, the statutory law must yield to fundamental law and be held void.

The Chief Justice in his opinion sustained this conclusion not only on general principles controlling the action of a court under a written Constitution limiting legislative powers, but he enforced it by reference to the express language of the Constitution itself in respect to the Court's jurisdiction and the supremacy of the Constitution.   This decision thus made the Judicial branch of the government the branch which could effectively determine the limits of power of the other two branches.   It became a precedent for similar action by courts in all the states, and for more than one hundred years it has been accepted as authoritative. Jefferson denounced it as usurpation of Judicial power. Every once in a while we have a recurrence of this criticism.   Such an attack figured very prominently in the general onslaught on courts that was made by the Progressive Party in agitating recall of judges and recall of judicial decisions.

The conclusion as to the invalidity of the law under which the petition for mandamus in Marbury *vs*. Madison was filed disposed of the case.   The Chief Justice, however, was not content to allow the case to go off in this way. Before deciding the question of jurisdiction, he seized the opportunity to pass upon the merits of the issue by deciding that if the Court had jurisdiction, it must issue the writ and compel Mr. Madison to deliver the Commission. He said that this was a duty of the Secretary which did not involve any discretion after the appointment had been made and the Commission had been signed and sent him for delivery. Such an expression of opinion was what the lawyers call *obiter dictum*. It was not necessary to the decision of the case before the Court. It was prompted by the political feelings of the Chief Justice and his colleagues and a willingness to criticize Madison and Jefferson. Here was the beginning of that long duel between Marshall and Jefferson. Marshall stood for the broad, liberal Federalistic construction of the Constitution, treating it as the expression of the whole people of the United States in founding a nation, while Jefferson insisted that it was nothing but a league of the independent states granting limited and delegated powers to a weak central government. Jefferson's term of office continued for eight years. He was followed by Madison and then by Monroe, over both of whom he seems to have exercised influence. Meantime Marshall continued on the Supreme Bench and lived ten years after Jefferson. Jefferson was the father, and until he died in 1825, the real head, of a great party which, with but a few short intervals, continued in power until the Civil War. Yet Marshall, a Federalist, in his service of more than a third of a century at the head of the Court, was able to breathe into the Constitution the spirit of nationality and of Federal supremacy so effectively that a court of Democrats succeeding him did not destroy his work. Marshall's construction of the Constitution is the fundamental law to-day, acquiesced in by all.

Both Marshall and Jefferson were great men. Marshall was probably the greatest judge that ever lived, when one considers the wonderful cogency and beauty of his judicial style, his statesman's foresight, the accuracy of his legal learning, the power of his reasoning, his soundness of judgment, his wonderful personal influence over his colleagues and the fateful influence of his work upon the structure of our great government. Jefferson had profound confidence in the people, and was the embodiment of the democratic principle. He was a genius in many ways. He was a voluminous and enormously industrious correspondent. He was a student of government and a statesman, a lawyer, an architect, a politician, a man of widest interests and information, the champion of all freedom and especially of religious tolerance, the founder of the University of Virginia, and a great promoter of education in that early day.

Though unnecessary to the decision, the principle of law laid down by Marshall in Marbury *vs.* Madison as to the right of a court to command the head of a department to do a ministerial duty, involving the exercise of no discretion, has been followed by the Supreme Court in several cases. In one case Congress directed that the Postmaster General credit certain contractors with the government with amounts to be ascertained by accounting officers. The Postmaster General refused to do this, and the Supreme Court held that a mandamus would lie to compel him to do it. In another case, the case of Decatur *vs.* Paulding, Congress had provided a pension for men and officers in the navy, to be granted by the Secretary of the Navy. Decatur's widow claimed that she was entitled to the pension under the law, and asked the Court to rule that she was thus entitled and to direct the Secretary of the Navy to allow her the pension. The Court held that in this case under the law Congress intended to entrust the granting of the pension to the official judgment of the Secretary of the Navy and that the Court would not control such Executive discretion. The distinction is to be found in the purpose of Congress. If that which remains to be done by the Executive officer does not involve and was not intended by Congress to involve discretion in doing it on the part of the Executive, then the courts can compel the Executive to do the act, but if any discretion is entrusted to the Executive, then the court is powerless. In the reconstruction period, after the Civil War, when Congress passed an act enabling the President to institute a military government in each of the conquered seceding states, suits were brought to enjoin the President from carrying out the law, on the ground that the law was invalid. The Court refused to enjoin the President, on the ground that even if the law was unconstitutional, the function of the President under the law was a political one with which the Court could not interfere, and this view was further enforced by the admitted impotency of the Court to restrain the President from carrying out the law if he believed it to be constitutional. This field of Judicial control over Executive action and the line between it and that in which there is no such control, offers an opportunity for the study of nice distinctions which I shall not, for lack of space, further pursue.

The President has power to convene Congress in extraordinary session, and to adjourn Congress when the Houses disagree as to adjournment, to such time as he may think proper.

When I convened Congress in extraordinary session to pass the Reciprocity bill, the leaders of the Democratic majority in the House were fearful that the Senate might attempt to adjourn after the bill was passed, and that the House might not have the opportunity of enacting some tariff bills for political use in the next election. The Democratic leaders therefore came to me to know whether I intended to exercise the power of adjourning the House in case of a disagreement. It had been reported that that was my plan. I had never thought of it and was able to assure them of this.

In a recent controversy between the Houses as to adjournment, an appeal was made to President Wilson to adjourn them. This power of prorogation, I was inclined to think when I was in the White House, was limited to the adjournment of an extra session of Congress, but I did not give the question full consideration. As I read it now, I think that the power of adjournment where the Houses differ over the question of adjournment can be exercised by the President at any session of Congress. No President has ever attempted to use this power.

The constitutional functions of the President seem very broad, and they are. When many speak of his great power, they have in mind that what the President does, goes, like kissing, by favor. I beg of you to believe that the Presidency offers but few opportunities for showing power of this sort. The responsibility of the office is so heavy, the earnest desire that every man who fills the place has to deserve the approval of his countrymen by doing the thing that is best for the country is so strong, and the fear of just popular criticism is so controlling, that it is difficult for one who has borne the burden of the office for four years to remember more than a few favors that he was able to confer. There are certain political obligations that the custom of a party requires the President to discharge on the recommendation of Senators and Congressmen. I hope to point out in the next chapter how that kind of obligation should be reduced to a minimum by a change of law. I refer now, however, to a different kind of power with which popular imagination clothes the President, that of gratifying one man, humiliating another, or punishing a third, in order to satisfy the pleasure, the whim or vengeance of a ruler. That does not exist. The truth is that great as his powers are, when a President comes to exercise them, he is much more concerned with the limitations upon them than he is affected, like little Jack Horner, by a personal joy over the big personal things he can do.

The President is given the White House to live in, —a very comfortable, homelike house. In all the world, I venture to say, there is no more appropriate official residence for a chief executive, or one better adapted to the simple democratic taste of the American people, than the White House. It is dignified, it is beautiful, it is commodious. It offers an opportunity for proper entertainment of the President's guests. It is much less extensive and much less ornate than the royal palaces of Europe, yet it is quite ample to surround the occupant with that dignified freedom from intrusion which the President ought to have.

There is an impression that the President cannot leave the country and that the law forbids. This is not true. The only law which bears on the subject at all is the constitutional provision that the Vice-President shall take his place when the President is disabled from performing his duties. Now if he is out of the country at a point where he cannot discharge the necessary functions that are imposed upon him, such disability may arise, but the communication by telegraph, wireless and by telephone are now so good that it would be difficult for a President to go anywhere out of the country and not be able to keep his subordinates in constant information as to his whereabouts and his wishes. As a custom, Presidents do not leave the country. Occasionally it seems in the public interest that he should. President Roosevelt visited the Canal Zone for the purpose of seeing what work was being done there and giving zest to it by personal contact with those who were engaged in it. I did the same thing later on, traveling, as he did, on the deck of a government vessel, which is technically the soil of the United States, from Hampton Roads to the Canal Zone under the dominion of the United States. We were not out of the jurisdiction except for a few hours. He went into the City of Panama, as I did, and dined with the President of the Panamanian Republic. So, too, I dined with President Diaz at Juarez in Mexico, just across the border from El Paso. Nobody was heard to say that in any of these visits we had disabled ourselves from performing our constitutional and statutory functions.

The assassination of three Presidents led Congress to provide that the Chief of the Secret Service should furnish protection to the President as he moves about either in Washington or in the country at large. While President, I never was conscious of any personal anxiety in large crowds, and I have been in many of them. Yet the record is such that Congress would be quite derelict if it disregarded it. These guards are a great burden to the President. He never can go anywhere that he does not have to inflict upon those whom he wishes to visit the burden of their presence. It is a little difficult for him to avoid the feeling after a while that he is under surveillance rather than under protection. The Secret Service men are level-headed, experienced and of good manners, and they are wise in their methods. If a person is determined to kill a President and is willing to give up his life to do it, no such protection will save him. But desperate persons of this kind are very rare. The worst danger is from those who have lost part or all of their reason and whom the presence of the President in the immediate neighborhood excites. I may be mistaken, but it seems to me that with such experts as we now have, the assassination of President McKinley in Buffalo might possibly have been avoided. Under the practice that the secret service men now pursue in a public reception, a man with a hand in his pocket would not be permitted to approach within striking or shooting distance of the President. His holding a revolver under his handkerchief in his pocket would now be detected long before he could get within reach of the object of his perverted purpose. He would find the hand of the Secret Service man thrust into the pocket to find what his own was doing there. Had this been done in the case of the assassin at Buffalo, that tragedy would probably not have occurred.

The President so fully represents his party, which secures political power by its promises to the people, and the whole government is so identified in the minds of the people with his personality that they are inclined to make him responsible for all the sins of omission and of commission of society at large. This would be ludicrous if it did not have sometimes serious results. The President cannot make clouds to rain and cannot make the corn to grow, he cannot make business good ; although when these things occur, political parties do claim some credit for the good things that have happened in this way. He has no power over state legislation, which covers a very wide field and which comes in many respects much closer to the happiness of the people than the Federal government.

Some urge, because the states have not shown themselves as active as they ought to be in suppressing evils and accomplishing good, that the United States government should thereby acquire additional authority, and the President and Congress should assume new functions. This would break up our whole Federal System. The importance of that system is frequently misunderstood. Its essence is in the giving through the states local control to the people over local affairs and confining national and general subjects to the direction of the central government. Our experience with the administration of the public lands, with the control of our national mineral wealth, with the irrigation system of arid lands which we have undertaken, and with the disposition of the many sources of water power owned by the United States, all show that it is exceedingly difficult for the central government to administer what in their nature are local matters and put in force a uniform national policy as to these subjects that may often be at variance with the local view. A centralized system of government, in which the President and Congress regulated the doorsteps of the people of this country, would break up the Union in a short time. Those who lightly call for this extension really do not understand the dangerous proposition they are urging.

While the President's powers are broad, the lines of his jurisdiction are as fixed as a written constitution can properly make them. He has tremendous responsibilities. Every President does the best he can, and while we may differ with him in judgment, while we may think he does not bring the greatest foresight to his task, while we may think that he selects poor instruments for his assistants and therefore we may properly vote against his reëlection to the office, we must remember that while he is in office, he is the head of our government. We should indulge in his favor the presumption that he acts under a high sense of duty. Correct ideals and disciplined intelligence should impose a special responsibility on men and women as law-abiding American citizens to be respectful to constituted authority and to the President, because it was the American people who chose him, and for the time being he is the personal embodiment and representative of their dignity and majesty.

CHAPTER III

The Power of Appointment

One of the functions which in a practical way gives the President more personal influence than any other is that of appointments. The prestige that a President has in the outset of his administration is in part due to this power. Even in the case of the most popular President, his prestige wanes with Congress as the term wears on and the offices are distributed. Mr. Evarts, in referring to filling consular places, said, "Some we appointed and more we disappointed." "'Tis true, 'tis pity, and pity 'tis, 'tis true."

Under the Constitution, Ambassadors, Public Ministers, Consuls, Judges of the Supreme Court and other officers of the United States, whose appointment is not otherwise provided for, are to be appointed by the President, with the advice and consent of the Senate. Congress is permitted to vest the appointment of inferior officers in the President alone, in the courts of law or in the heads of departments. Heads of departments could hardly be called inferior officers — at least they would object to such an interpretation — though Senators and Congressmen sometimes call them so. The language of the Constitution thus leaves it doubtful whether Congress could give the selection of his Cabinet to the President without confirmation by the Senate. The question will not trouble us, however, for the Senate is never likely to consent to waive the right it now has, to pass upon the President's choice of his official family.

As a matter of fact, all the important offices, and a great many offices that are not important, in addition to the ones especially mentioned in the Constitution, are filled by the President, by and with the advice and consent of the Senate. The President alone is authorized by Congress to appoint comparatively few officers. There are minor officers in great number, notably the fourth-class postmasters, that are appointed by the head of a department. The Clerks of the courts and the United States Commissioners are appointed by the judges of the respective courts.

It was settled, as long ago as the first Congress, at the instance of Madison, then in the Senate, and by the deciding vote of John Adams, then Vice-President, that even where the advice and consent of the Senate was necessary to the appointment of an officer, the President had the absolute power to remove him without consulting the Senate. This was on the principle that the power of removal was incident to the Executive power and must be untrammeled. In the administration of Andrew Johnson, the Republican Congress regarded the President as an apostate and a traitor to Republican principles. With a two-thirds majority in each House, it sought to reverse this principle as to the power of removal by the tenure of office act. Its first section continued a person in an office in which he had been confirmed by the Senate, until the appointment and qualification of his successor. This of course made his removal dependent upon the advice and consent of the Senate to the appointment of a successor, and put the question of removal, therefore, completely within the control of the Senate. The act further especially provided that the head of a department should hold his office during the term of the President who appointed him, and should be subject to removal only by consent of the Senate. This grew out of Mr. Johnson's removal of Mr. Stanton from the War Office. When President Grant came into office, much of the act was repealed at his instance. It never came before the courts directly in such a way as to invite a decision on its validity, but there are intimations in the opinions of the Supreme Court that in the tenure of office act Congress exceeded its legislative discretion.

As we look back upon the history of Johnson's administration, and can remember the extreme and passionate feeling entertained by good, moral, patriotic men toward Mr. Johnson, and the measures to which they were willing to resort in order to deprive him of his official power, and indeed of his office, we have a most significant illustration of the wisdom of limitations in a written Constitution, imposed by a highly intelligent people in their calm and deliberative moments upon action which may be taken by themselves under the influence of passion and prejudice. Now that the period has become history, and a half century passed, we realize that it would have been a blot upon the fairness of the American people to have removed Mr. Johnson, with all his temperamental defects, on the grounds charged in the impeachment articles, and we rejoice that there were dissentient Republicans enough to prevent the majority of votes in favor of the impeachment from reaching the necessary two-thirds. It was a great deal better to put up with the gross mistakes involved in Mr. Johnson's policies from a Republican point of view, than it was by a strained and unfair construction of the Constitution and of the evidence advanced, to remove him from his office on the ground that he had committed high crimes and misdemeanors in its administration. It is useful to dwell on this one of many notable instances in the history of every popular government, to refute the proposition upon which the recall of judges, the recall of judicial decisions, the attack upon written Constitutions and upon the system of their judicial interpretation and enforcement is based. That proposition is that because the people have and ought to have the power to adopt the written Constitution and to amend it, therefore they are fitted to interpret and apply the Constitution, and in effect amend it, in a particular case between particular individuals. This is an egregious fallacy. The best and most intelligent men, well able wisely to frame and adopt a written Constitution laying down general limitations, in accordance with general principle, nevertheless may, and often do, lose their fairness and clearness of vision over a special case between special individuals arousing personal or party passion.

According to the last report of the United States Civil Service Commission, the number of officers and employees in the executive civil service, on the 30th of June, 1913, was 469,879. With the increase in the offices which occurred in the last Congress, and with the actual increase that follows the growth of the population, it will soon be half a million. By the activities of these civil servants, the Federal government maintains its personal presence, so to speak, in every local community throughout the vast stretch of national jurisdiction. In the days before the present civil service law, a sense of obligation to the President for the places held, made practically all the civil employees his political henchmen. In those halcyon times, even the humblest charwoman or the most poorly paid janitor felt a throb of deep personal interest in the political health of the President.

Machine politics and the spoils system are as much an enemy of a proper and efficient government system of civil service as the boll weevil is of the cotton crop, or the various forms of insects and blight are of the farmer and the horticulturist in their pursuits. The strength of these pernicious influences has not been entirely destroyed by the present Federal civil service law. I think, however, their evil has been more mitigated in the Federal civil service system than in the states where there is a merit system. In the rush of reform in the last decade, I believe nine of the states have adopted the competitive civil service system and a requirement for its adoption has been incorporated in the charters of 250 cities. The Federal system, is older and much better enforced. The difficulty, however, that we encounter is the same as in the carrying out of many reforms. The securing of the necessary legislation proves to be only a necessary initial step, but perhaps not the most important and difficult one. The law will not enforce itself. It has accomplished one purpose in enabling those who voted for it in the legislature to claim credit for it on the stump. But such a law cannot be drawn, which will be practical, and at the same time will not permit evasion of its purpose by a politician in the executive chair who devotes his time to it. We often therefore find the law more honored in the breach than in the observance. The life of a civil service system on the merit principle is in its executive enforcement, and that only comes with a gradual improvement in the public scrutiny and the official conscience in respect to the law. If a party remains in power for a number of successive terms, the merit system acquires a stronger hold than where frequent changes from one party to another in the executive administration tempt the seizure of patronage for party purposes by hook or crook. Still we should not be disheartened. Defective as the Federal system law has proved to be in certain ways, the principle has made great headway since it was adopted in 1883. The positions then affected by it numbered about 14,000. On June 30th, 1913, the positions affected were more than 282,000, and of these 172,000 were brought under the law by executive orders extending the system, while 110,000 were included by the natural expansion of the service after the orders had become effective. About 190,000 positions under the government are not subject to competitive examination. Of these 10,000 are Presidential appointees. The remainder are laborers or contracting employees whose exclusion from the classified service is doubtless justified by the conditions. It is with respect to the 10,000 Presidential employees that a real improvement can be brought about. They are most of them local Federal officers distributed throughout the United States, first, second and third class postmasters, collectors of customs, collectors of internal revenue and public land officers. They must be confirmed by the Senate. Where an appointment is subject to confirmation by the Senate, it cannot by executive order be put in the classified civil service. Congress might, however, repeal the necessity for confirmation and give the appointments to the President alone. He then could classify them all and incorporate them in the merit system, and the appointments to such places would be filled by promotions from subordinate positions of assistants. Thus all the local offices throughout the country, the postmasters, the collectors of internal revenue, the collectors of customs, and all other subordinates, would be given permanent tenure and appointed and promoted after examination and upon proved efficiency. The retention by Congress of the necessity for confirmation by the Senate enables members to keep these local offices out of the classified service, and to make them the football of politics. In effect, it enables them to administer these offices as personal patronage, under a custom which is established through the so-called courtesy of the Senate. Under it, the partisan majority in the Senate will usually decline to confirm an appointment made by the President to a postmastership or a collectorship, which is not recommended by the Senators or Congressmen from the district in which the appointee lives and is to discharge his duties. There is a clear understanding between Senators and Congressmen as to how this patronage is to be divided between them in each state, and the President attempting to break up the custom has heretofore found himself unable to do so.

There have been notable instances, as in the case of President Garfield and Senators Conkling and Platt, where the President asserted his right to act without the recommendation of the New York Senators in a New York appointment. Public sympathy ran with the President in this controversy, as it generally does, but tradition and the advantage of cohesion in the Senate make it difficult to overcome the custom. More than this, in the Garfield-Conkling controversy, it was not a question of civil service reform. The issue was political. It was only a question whether a Conkling man should be replaced by a Blaine man, and it was a question whether Mr. Garfield should be permitted to pay a political debt of Mr. Blaine by the appointment of Mr. Blaine's friend, Judge Robertson, and the removal of a friend of Senator Conkling. Nor did Mr. Garfield seek to change the custom except in this case. In one of his state papers he expressly advocated the system of recommendations for such appointments by Congressmen and Senators. From time to time in the present administration, there have been threatened issues over confirmations between the President and the Senate, growing out of party factional differences, but they have been smoothed over, and I think it will be found generally that the Senate has maintained the custom of which I have spoken. An attempt on the President's part to break up the custom would create a factional opposition which would interfere with the passing of the bills he recommends, and endanger the successful carrying out of the policies to which he is pledged.

Any discussion of the subject is lacking which does

not make some reference to the solemn argument of
solemn Senators in the effort to enlarge the meaning
of the words "advice and consent of the Senate", used
by the Constitution in describing the part the Senate
should play in the matter of appointments. The
usual contention is that these words require that
the President, before making a nomination, consult
the Senate. To use Skipper Jack Bunsby's language,
as reported in *Dombey and Son*, "The bearings of
this observation is in the application on it." Such a
construction of the term "advice and consent" easily
leads one imbued with the sacred awfulness of the
Senate's function in the government to the conclusion
that a Republican President under the Constitution
and the courtesy of the Senate must consult the
Republican Senators from a state before making an
appointment in that state, although no such constitutional or statutory obligation is upon him in respect of
Democratic Senators. The Constitution thus varies
in its application to the power of Senators of one political party and to the Senators of another. This is not
entirely humorous, much as it may seem to be. A Senator asked me to appoint two men, one to be District
Attorney, and the other his assistant, and requested that
they be allowed to divide the aggregate salary of the two
offices equally. When I declined to do so, he requested
the appointment of one of them to the chief office.
Upon investigation, I did not think his standing at the
bar was such as to justify the appointment, and was
confirmed in this opinion by his willingness to accept the
office under the arrangement as suggested. I nominated another lawyer of much higher capacity and

greater fitness, who was also a political supporter of the Senator. He fought the nomination on the ground that with devilish ingenuity I had sought to embarrass him. While he admitted the competency and high character of my nominee and his proper political views, he argued that as his advice to me had been different, and as he in such local matters represented the Senate, and had not advised and consented to the nomination, the appointment should not be confirmed, in his view of the constitutional function of the Senate in appointments. I should, in fairness, say that the Senate did not sanction his view.

As long as these important local offices remain political, and are the patronage of Senators and Congressmen, the expense of the administration of the offices will be largely more than it need be. I was much interested during my term of office in devising a system for the permanent promotion of efficiency and economy in the government service. I induced Congress to give me $100,000 a year for two years, to pay the expenses of an expert Commission, to examine the governmental business and make reports upon the changes needed by the introduction of modern business methods and economy, to enable the people to get more for their money. The reports that they made, by which they pointed out needed changes in our present system, including the budget, which I described in my first chapter, were not popular with Congress, especially not with the last Congress of my term. The necessary appropriation was withdrawn. The Commission, however, did a great deal of most useful work, and while the dust is accumulating on their reports at present, their investigations and conclusions were of permanent value, and some day they will be made the basis for further investigation and for definite measures of reform. Among other conclusions which they reached, and which makes a reference to their work relevant here, was that the requirement for confirmation by the Senate of these local Federal offices, numbering about 10,000, should be repealed, and that the force in all the offices should be reclassified, and all, including the chief officers, should be put in the classified service. They reported that if this was done, the chief offices might be abolished and the work be done by the present assistants, whose salaries could be increased 20 per cent. In this way the work of the government would be more effectively done by the assistants who are usually experts, and there would be a saving of $4,500,000 a year.

Not only would the government's business be better done, but there would be eliminated opportunity for the use of Federal appointments to influence or control political nominations and elections, an abuse which has greatly helped the maintenance of machine politics and the success of professional political positions. I recommended such a change in my four annual messages, but Congress took no notice of the suggestion. Congressmen and Senators have an impression that to lose this patronage would very seriously interfere with their political future and power. I do not mean to say that some Congressmen and some Senators do not make such patronage politically useful for themselves, but I venture to think, and the judgment of men of much greater political experience and observation than I have had will sustain me, that the having, and use of, such patronage more often injures than helps the user in securing his renomination and reëlection. It is a saying in Washington, justified by the fact, that an appointment of a first, second, third or fourth class postmaster not infrequently creates for the Congressman who secures it one ingrate and ten enemies.

Candor compels me to refer to some dangers in our extension of the classified service and permanent tenure of employees. Substantial progress toward better things can rarely be taken without developing new evils requiring new remedies. In the classified system, there are large bodies of mail carriers, postal mail clerks, and of other subordinate civil servants, who have a common interest in an increase in their salary or other terms of their employment. They form associations or in effect trades-unions. They perfect their organizations. They publish a newspaper. Their government duties carry them into close contact with the people and voters of the various Congressional districts, and in indirect ways they seek to bring undue political pressure upon the members of Congress and the Senate to accomplish their personal desires. They are often successful in this. It is a pernicious use of the opportunities given by their official duties to secure an advance of their pay or other more favorable terms of service, on other grounds than the merit of the question. Executive orders have been issued to prevent such activities, but the demagogues of both Houses and both parties rush forward to hamper Executive authority in this respect, and the evil thus far has continued. It has been used as an argument against the classified competitive system. It seems to me the

proper view to take of this is that we must find some
means to prevent such an abuse, but that it should
not be a reason for losing the great advantage of the
merit system.

I cannot exaggerate the waste of the President's
time and the consumption of his nervous vitality involved in listening to Congressmen's intercession as to
local appointments. Why should the President have
his time taken up in a discussion over the question who
shall be postmistress at the town of Devil's Lake in
North Dakota? How should he be able to know, with
confidence, who is best fitted to fill such a place? If we
were to follow ordinary business methods in a matter
which concerns business only and does not concern general political policies, as we ought to do, would we not
leave such appointments to the natural system of promotion for efficiency? If the persons and parties contending for the abolition of bosses and the suppression
of machines would show the faith and sincerity that
ought to be in them, they could promote the cause which
they so loudly proclaim, most effectively, by passing the
law which I recommended to Congress. Votes upon such
a measure would be a test of their sincerity in this matter.
I regret to say that up to this time, few members of any
party, whether Republican, Democratic or Progressive,
however drastic reformers, have stood this test. Of
course there were machines that were corrupt and there
were bosses that made a profession of politics and held
themselves out as political attorneys to be retained.
There are not so many now. A great reform in this
respect has been effected. But parties are essential to
the success of popular government, and parties mean

organization. It is not without humor to note the effect upon the enthusiastic purist and reformer in politics when a consciousness of this steals over him, and he begins to look with tenderness upon the use of patronage to help the organization of the party which was founded in the interest of pure reform. We find that often the difference between political machines and a party organization for reform is only determined by the question, "Is it for you or against you?" If it is for you and your ideas, it is a justifiable organization, and the more effective you can make it, the better. If it is against you, it is a low political machine and ought to be condemned out of the mouths of all decent people. If the leader of the organization is with you, he is a political leader with a statesmanlike view. If he is against you, he is a boss, and the typical head of a dangerous machine. This personal element and this distinction between the evil use of patronage and the good use of patronage are the two obstructions to a betterment of our civil service system. Everything that tends to arbitrary and complete power in any officer in the distribution of offices, whose duties do not affect the determination of political policies, is demoralizing. It gives sanction to favoritism, and favoritism develops abuses even where its exercise is entrusted to the best men.

The law puts the appointment of clerks of courts in the judges. Judges are men of high character, great ability and wide learning generally, but when they are given executive or quasi-political functions, that is, when they exercise patronage, they have proven to be quite like other men. Clerks appointed in the Federal district courts become part of the family of the judge.

Their appointments are practically for life. They feel secure. They are close to the judge. Their associations are intimate. They naturally seek to increase the earnings of their offices, especially when their salaries are more or less dependent on the amount of their official earnings, and they are prone to overcharges. The favor they enjoy with the judge as part of his family has, I am sorry to say, permitted such abuses. The reluctance that some judges have to call their clerks to strict account in the management of their offices is too well known to the head of the Department of Justice, and to his inspectors, whose duty it is to examine their accounts. When in office, I recommended that the President have the power of removal of such clerks for cause, upon the report of the Attorney-General, but no such action was taken, although there were a number of cases presented justifying such a change in the law. With nearly one hundred clerks of courts, and with a larger number of deputies spread all over the United States, the influence that can be used with members of Congress in a matter like this, not acutely political, only those who have had occasion to meet it can fully understand.

In order to protect the judges against their unjudicial selves in extra judicial matters, I would remove all patronage from the courts. The patronage of the Lord Chancellor in England is very large indeed, and it does not tend to the higher standing of that great judicial officer. Lord Westbury, one of the ablest Chancellors England ever had, was compelled to resign because of a difficulty growing out of the patronage which he had exercised in behalf of a member of his family who had abused his office. I would vest the appointment of receivers in equity to take charge of railroads by the Federal courts in the Interstate Commerce Commission. They could be made of course quite as subject to the direction of the court, though appointed by another authority, as if appointed by the court itself. I know whereof I speak as to the wisdom of such a change. For eight years I acted as a circuit judge, and during much of that time, I was engaged through receivers in operating many thousands of railroads within my circuit. The executive power of appointment the court is thus called upon to exercise is not good for the court, creates antagonisms that ought to be avoided, and interferes with the proper discharge of normal judicial functions. The vesting in courts of the appointment of supervisors of election under the Federal election laws before their repeal was greatly detrimental to the standing of the Federal courts and necessarily had the effect to drag them into partisan controversy. In the South, because the judges were generally of the opposite political complexion from that of the great body of the voters, it made the courts for the time being alien courts. Since the abolition of the Federal election laws and the appointments of a number of Democratic judges in the South, I think the standing of the Federal courts with the people of that section has become changed for the better.

In my judgment, the President should not be required to exercise his judgment to make appointments except to fill the most important offices. In the Executive department, he should be limited to the selection of those officers, the discharge of whose duties involves discretion in the carrying out of the political and governmental policy of his administration. He therefore ought to have the appointment of his Cabinet officers, and he ought also to have the appointment of a political under-secretary in each department to take the place of the head of the department when for any reason the head of the department is not able to discharge his usual duties. All other officers in the departments, including the Assistant Secretaries and the Chiefs of Bureaus, should have a permanent tenure and not change with each administration. This would greatly facilitate the continuity of the government and prevent the halt and lack of efficiency that necessarily attend a change in the Assistant Secretaries in each department and in the Chiefs of all Bureaus. For a year or a year and a half, at least, sometimes for a longer period, it throws the administration of the department into the complete control of minor subordinates, the Chiefs of Divisions and Chief Clerks, and makes the inexperienced heads of departments, Assistant Secretaries and Chiefs of Bureaus entirely dependent on such subordinates.

Consider the entirely unnecessary helplessness of our government in the administration of our foreign relations, in which there is a greater necessity for continuity of policy than in any other department, when men having no practical knowledge of the previous foreign policy of the government, its safe traditions or of diplomatic custom, are substituted for competent officials. When such changes are possible, we put ourselves at a great disadvantage in dealing with the departments of foreign affairs of other countries, and this disadvantage is accentuated and increased when competent representatives abroad in our diplomatic service are removed and men of no experience replace them. The President of course should appoint the Supreme Judges, as the Constitution requires, and the inferior judges of the Federal judiciary. He ought, too, to appoint the general officers of the army and the flag officers of the navy, and he ought also to appoint the leading Ambassadors and Ministers. Other appointments, it seems to me, might well be left to a system of promotion, to be carried on under civil service rules as interpreted and enforced by a Commission and the heads of departments. In this way, the attention of the President would be taken up in matters of appointment with those offices in which he would have a full opportunity to learn of the qualifications of proper candidates, and in the appointment of which, because of the conspicuous importance of the duties to be discharged, he would be held to a proper responsibility by a much more discriminating public scrutiny than can possibly be exercised in respect to the less important and subordinate offices.

I have spoken of the drain upon the nervous vitality of the President in the consideration of the many subordinate offices that he has to fill and the constant interviews that he is bound to have with Congressmen and with Senators over such appointments, and the disputes and friction incident to the decision in such cases. One cannot go through the strain of the Presidential office, especially in such cases, unless he has a sense of humor. That takes up the jolts, and it lightens the monotonous and annoying routine and gives an opportunity for a study of the play of motives in human nature. No one has as good opportunity to know Senators and Congressmen as the President, because in asking the Presidential favor, the Senator or Congressman frequently bares his motives and discloses his inmost traits of character in the confidence and secrecy of the Executive office. It is more or less an unconscious confessional. It enables the President to measure the characters of men in public life. He finds that some popular idols have feet of clay, and that others not held in great public esteem have sturdier virtues and more disinterested anxiety for the public weal than their press-made reputations would indicate.

Sometimes the incidents are farcical and mirthmaking. I remember one case of the wife of a politician of influence, who was anxious to secure an appointment for her son. She procured the recommendation of Congressmen and Senators in both parties, and to see that they said what she wished them to say, she accompanied them to the Executive office. When the appointment, which was for a technical place, was given to another, she wrote me a letter, most severe, in which she arraigned me for ingratitude in not giving her permanent happiness, as I might, by the turn of my hand, when she had secured a number of votes for a bill in the passage of which I was much interested as an administration measure. I wrote to her in as gentle a way as possible to break the blow to a mother's heart and supposed that the incident was closed ; but an accidental delay in the confirmation led to the writing of a letter in the name of her husband, but in her handwriting, in which I was advised that she was seriously ill in bed with a disease usually fatal and which was injuriously affected by the mental worry which I had given her by a failure to make the appointment which she sought. The letter requested that I withdraw the name which had been sent in and appoint her son in order that she might rise again from what otherwise would be her last illness. I wrote another sympathetic letter explaining why this could not be done. The appointment I had made was confirmed immediately after, and within two days this lady and her husband were the first guests to greet Mrs. Taft and me at a White House musicale, without the slightest evidence of any illness at all, and with an attractive smile which seemed to say, "That episode is ended and we are on good terms still."

A lady of charming appearance and manner, elegantly gowned, came to me when I was Secretary of War, and asked that her son be admitted to West Point. The son had been appointed, but had failed to pass the entrance examinations. I explained to her why we had to be very careful in making our examinations as stiff as we dared to make them because the benefit and advantage of an appointment to West Point, which gave a fine education, and during which the cadets received a salary from the government, justified a test eliminating the unworthy. She rather impatiently asked me to examine the papers, which I did, and found to my surprise that her son had passed an examination in which he had obtained a mark of 95 out of 100. This was unusual and commended him strongly to me. I found that his rejection had been on the ground that his chest measurement did not bear such a ratio to his height, which was great, as the medical board had thought to be proper and necessary. I explained to the lady the necessity that we were under of having strong and healthy boys educated at West Point, because if there was anything organically the trouble with them which might develop later, the government ran the risk of being obliged to retire such men for disability and to pay them three-fourths pay all their lives without receiving any compensatory service. She listened to this explanation with a lack of attention and a nervous restlessness which husbands will understand. An examination of the papers, however, made me feel that, as we needed men of brains as well as brawn in the army, the unusual mental capacity would justify my running the risk of the boy's filling out his chest measurements to the required extent. I said to the mother therefore that as I had no difficulty in filling out my chest measurement, I thought it would be possible for her son, with his intellectual capacity, to follow a regimen to give his lungs the proper room, and that I was inclined to waive the objections. She did not quite follow me in my statement and she inquired eagerly, "Are you going to let him in?" I said I was, and then there spread over her comely face a rosy smile, and she hesitated a moment to think what she could say to express her gratitude and her satisfaction with me, and then she said, "Mr. Secretary, you are not nearly so fat as they say you are." A recollection of that remark has enabled me to get through a good many scenes that were much more annoying and had a much less satisfactory issue.

The framers of our Constitution had one essential feature of efficient government clearly in mind. They gave to the Executive officer charged in law with the responsibility and actually charged by the people with the responsibility of carrying on the Executive department of the government, the power and means of meeting that responsibility. They vested in him complete power to appoint all the officers of the government who were subordinate to him, and upon whose political capacity and governmental discretion would depend the wise carrying out of his policies. They gave him the power of absolute removal, and they placed in his hands the control of the action of all those who took part in the discharge of the political duties of the executive department. They acted on a sound political principle, and it ought to be introduced into every field of governmental activity, into the states and into the cities. The plan under which a dozen state officers engaged in executing the laws are elected on one ticket and have no relation of subordination to the normal executive head, the governor, is as absurd as it can be. It is one of those anomalies in our political history, of which there are a number, which seem to refute the idea that we are an intelligent and clear-sighted people, because the system adopted is so utterly at variance with the teachings of experience. But we have had such governments — indeed most of our state governments are of this kind. They have not been as good governments as they might have been or as they ought to have been, and yet they have worked. The fact that they have worked, may properly be taken as the most conclusive evidence of the political capacity of the

American people through public opinion to maintain a fairly good government and to get along somehow, with what seems *a priori* to be an impossible system. The Constitutional Convention has recommended a change in the present form of the government of New York, which is a most flagrant example in its plan of what a state government ought not to be. They have reduced the number of elective officers to four, on the principle of what is called the short ballot, and they have put the seventeeen departments of the state under the executive control of the governor. This is as it should be, and is a step forward of such notable and radical character that the change that it would make alone is enough to justify the adoption of the proposed Constitution.

CHAPTER IV

The Duty of the President to take Care that the Laws are Executed. The Power and Duties of the President as Commander-in-Chief

The widest power and the broadest duty which the President has is conferred and imposed by a clause in section three of article two, providing that "he shall take care that the laws be faithfully executed." This same duty is enforced by the provision that before he enter on the execution of his office, he shall take the following oath or affirmation:

I do solemnly swear or affirm that I will faithfully execute the office of President of the United States, and will to the best of my ability, preserve, protect and defend the Constitution of the United States.

In executing a statute of Congress, through the proper department and the proper subordinate officers, the President's course is as clear, or as doubtful, as the statute. In order that he or his subordinates shall enforce the statute, they must necessarily find out what it means, and on their interpretation of it enforce the law. Statutory construction is practically one of the greatest of executive powers. Some one has said, "Let me make the ballads of the country, and I care not who makes the laws." One might also say, paraphrasing this, "Let any one make the laws of the country, if I can construe them." Of course ultimately where a statute affects private right, it is likely to come before the courts in actual litigation and to put upon the courts the duty of its construction. But there are many statutes that do not affect private right in such a way that they come under the court's interpretation; and in such cases Executive interpretation is final. Even where it is not, it is very persuasive with courts who subsequently are obliged to adjudge the meaning of the statute.

In the practical provision for the enforcement of law by Congress, that body has found it necessary to impose upon the President or his subordinates not only a purely Executive function, but to enlarge this into what are really quasi-legislative and quasi-judicial duties. Frequently in statutes covering a wide field, Congress confers upon the particular subordinate of the President, who is to execute this law, the power to make rules and regulations under it which are legislative in their nature. This is for the purpose of enabling those who are affected by the terms of the law, both government officers and the public, to learn how it is to be enforced, and how it is to be complied with. If you would know the importance, difficulty and wide discretion involved in such a task, I commend you to the present income tax, and beg you to note "the main strength" that had to be used in formulating workable regulations for its operation and enforcement, and which were really a reconciliation of the parts of the law that seemed inconsistent and almost irreconcilable.

The Commissioner of Internal Revenue, with the approval of the Secretary of the Treasury, issues regulations for the collection of the internal revenue taxes generally. The customs laws are interpreted and supplemented by regulations of the Secretary of the Treasury. The Department of the Interior, in the administration of the land laws, has a book of regulations that are of a minor legislative character, and this is true of other bureaus and departments of the government in respect to laws to be enforced by them.

Congressional legislation often confers on those who comply with its conditions property rights or valuable privileges. Now Congress may exercise a choice as to whether it shall give jurisdiction to pass upon the claims of those seeking these rights to an Executive tribunal or a Judicial tribunal. The application for a patent for an invention is made to the Commissioner of Patents or a subordinate, but provision is made for an appeal from his decision to the Secretary of the Interior and thence to a court. Soldiers' pensions, however, and patents under the homestead and other general land laws for government lands, are granted upon application, after a hearing before an Executive tribunal, to determine whether the applicants come within the conditions of the act granting the pension or the land. Under the immigration acts are officers exercising similar quasi-judicial powers subject to review by the head of the department only, for the purpose of determining whether immigrants who come to this country are eligible under its laws to enter. The laws have now gone to the extent of providing that such tribunals may direct the deportation of those who have illegally entered, and that they may finally decide, after a fair hearing, whether a man claiming to be a citizen of the United States, and thus entitled to enter, is really such a citizen. This shows how judicial in its nature the function of the subordinates of the President in the execution of laws may become.

Then consider the drawing of money from the Treasury Department under an appropriation act. The drawing of the warrant must be approved by the Comptroller of the Treasury. It is for him to say how the appropriation act shall be construed and whether the warrant is lawful and whether the money can be drawn. The Comptroller of the Treasury is an appointee of the President, and in a general sense is his subordinate. If the President does not like him as a Comptroller, he can remove him and with the consent of the Senate put in another one, but under the act of Congress creating the office, the President cannot control or revise the decisions of this officer. His work is like the work I have referred to, quasi-judicial. If the claim is rejected by him, the claimant may in some cases carry his case into the Court of Claims, but if he decides for the claimant, the public and those interested in maintaining the side of the government have no appeal, and his decision is final.

Originally claims against the government could not be heard in court. The government did not permit itself to be sued, the claims were passed upon by Executive officers and were referred to Congress for its consideration and action by appropriation. Now a Court of Claims has been established with jurisdiction to hear and adjudge suits against the United States, based on contracts, express or implied, and in a narrow class of torts. Judgments in the Court of Claims are certified to Congress for payment and are subject to review by the Supreme Court of the United States. This development from the decision of executive officers from claims depending upon government concession or grants, into executive tribunals and finally into a real judicial hearing before a court, is one of numerous instances of the tendencies of the Anglo-Saxon to give a hearing as fair and equitable as is consistent with the effective operation of the government purpose. It was seen originally in the growth and development of the court of chancery out of the arbitrary decisions of the Lord Keeper in dealing with the litigants at common law, and ameliorating its rigidity. The creation of many executive Commissions has given rise to qualms in the minds of some, lest we are departing from those forms of proceeding intended to protect individual right. It may well be pointed out that the trend in all such executive tribunals is toward due judicial hearing and procedure.

The instances that I have been considering are cases of government concession. Of course in such cases it is entirely within the power of Congress to prescribe the conditions of granting the concession. When individuals are affected by act of Congress in their vested rights of life, liberty and property, then Congress is limited in conferring its method. One general limitation is that Congress may not deprive a person of his life, liberty or property except by due process of law. Therefore Congress may not confer on the Executive, judicial power, that is, power to decide cases that according to the due course of law should be heard by courts. Such are controversies of private right between individuals. Such are the trials of individuals for crimes. An executive may not be vested with the authority to decide such issues. This is the general rule, and yet custom and the due course at common law have created exceptions to this general rule, exceptions growing out of the inherent necessities of government. The collection of taxes deprives a man of his property by taking a part of it, but there is no limitation upon the legislative power requiring it to afford judicial settlement of the amount of taxes to be collected from an individual under uniform rules laid down by the legislature. The method must be summary. Congress may vest final decision as to their construction in any executive officer or board. Of course if the tax law violates the Constitution, then it is void and gives no officer any authority to act under it. But where the question is only one of construction, Congress may, in tax cases, keep it out of the courts entirely and vest final interpretation and execution in the taxing officer. Congress has not generally done this, but has ultimately given an opportunity for the taxpayer to appeal to the Federal courts. However, the United States always takes the money first. No injunction is permitted to suspend the agony of an unwilling taxpayer and permit him to withhold the money pending the deliberation of a court.

The express duties defined in the statute, and distributed to the departments and to the various appointees of the President, create a great permanent organization over which he can exercise only a very general supervision. Under the civil service laws, inadequate as they are in some respects, the continuity of the government in the departments at Washington in routine matters is fairly well settled and is little changed from administration to administration. It would be difficult, if the President chose to exercise the power he has, to impose his personality minutely on the going government. He can insist upon greater economy. He can infuse a new spirit in the service by making plain his earnest desire for greater efficiency, and yet while he is, of course, the real head of the government, there seems to be an impersonal entity in the permanent governmental structure, independent of him, which in some degree modifies his responsibility for its operation. Chiefs of Divisions and clerks of Bureaus in the civil service in Washington have been there for decades. They are loyal to the government, and not especially beholden to any one President. They are as important in the army of civil servants as the old non-commissioned officers are in a military force. They have far greater experience than the heads of their departments and bureaus who change every Presidential term. Their life-long fidelity and efficiency are not rewarded by notices in headlines. They have true philosophy, and are content with small salaries, permanent tenure, a conscience of duty well done and the flattering dependence upon them that their immediate superiors manifest. This permanent structure of government works on. Presidents may go to the seashore or to the mountains, Cabinet Officers may go about the country explaining how fortunate the country is in having such an administration, but the machinery at Washington continues to operate under this army of faithful non-commissioned officers, and the great mass of governmental business is un-interrupted. The President notes little of this normal operation of the regular vast machine of government, which in many respects is automatic, unless its work-ings result in a break or there is a palpable need of repair. The chief concern of the President is in following a path that is not so clearly beaten as the routine work done by this inconspicuous but necessary governmental machine which I have de-scribed.

The laws that the President must take care shall be faithfully executed are not confined to acts of Con-gress. The treaties of the United States with other countries are under the Constitution laws of the United States having the same effect as Congressional enact-ments, in so far as they are intended to operate in this way and are in form appropriate. Sometimes, how-ever, Congress does not like a treaty and refuses to pass a law to make compliance with it by the Execu-tive as easy at it ought to be. This was the case with the treaty which John Jay made with Great Britain. Jay was hung in effigy, and his work though ratified by the Senate and Washington was nearly as unpopular as the alien and sedition laws of a little later period.

Jay's Treaty provided that England and the United States on proper requisition from each to the other should deliver up all persons charged with murder or forgery, within the jurisdiction of one and seeking an asylum in the jurisdiction of the other. Congress during John Adams' administration passed no law to carry out this article and made no provision, as it has done since in all such cases, for any examination of the accused before a court as the basis for granting a warrant of extradition. No express power was given to the President to issue such a warrant. The matter stood on the naked words of the treaty. A subject of Great Britain committed a murder on the high seas on a British ship, and then escaped to South Carolina. He was there apprehended and brought before the Federal court for commitment on the charge of piracy in alleged violation of statutes of the United States. President Adams wrote to the examining judge that it did not seem to him that this was piracy and that the Federal court had no jurisdiction over the act as such; that the crime was murder and was committed within the jurisdiction of Great Britain and therefore was within the treaty; that the English government had requested the delivery of the accused under the treaty to their agent, and that if the judge found the evidence of the probable guilt of the prisoner sufficient, he, the President, would order him to be turned over to England. The judge agreed that there was no jurisdiction in the Federal court, but said that the evidence was sufficient for commitment on the charge of homicide. The President issued his warrant, the man was delivered to the English authorities and was tried and executed for his offense. Edward Livingston, one of the greatest jurists that ever lived in the United States, was then a Republican member of Congress and a follower of Jefferson, and a very strenuous political opponent of President Adams. He introduced resolutions which recited that the action of the President was an unjustifiable interference with the court's jurisdiction, that there was no statute authorizing an order of extradition by the President, and therefore that his act was a usurpation and a violation of the personal rights of the man who had been extradited and executed. John Marshall, afterwards Chief Justice, was then a member of the House of Representatives and a supporter of the administration. He made an argument to sustain the validity of President Adams' warrant. It is reported in the first appendix of the Fifth Wheaton. Mr. Justice Gray, speaking for the Supreme Court, nearly one hundred years later, pronounced the argument to be masterly and conclusive, and to establish that within the President's constitutional obligation to take care that the laws be faithfully executed, the treaty obligation of the United States was such a law. If you will read the argument of then Congressman Marshall, you will agree with the Court and Mr. Justice Gray. It is as convincing and as judicial in its tone as one of Chief Justice Marshall's great judgments.

A similar instance came within my own official cognizance when I was Secretary of War. In the absence of Mr. Root, Secretary of State, President Roosevelt sent me to Cuba to see if we could compose a revolution against President Palma's government in that Republic. We found a revolution flagrant, and we felt that intervention was necessary, and the question was whether the President, without action of Congress, could use the army and navy and intervene under the so-called Platt Amendment of the Treaty between Cuba and the United States. That Amendment was in part as follows:

The Government of Cuba' consents that the United States may exercise the right to intervene for the preservation of Cuban independence, and the maintenance of a government adequate for the protection of life, property, and individual liberty.

I advised the President that this treaty, *pro tanto*, extended the jurisdiction of the United States to maintain law and order over Cuba in case of threatened insurrection, and of danger of life, property and individual liberty, and that under his duty to take care that the laws be executed this was "a law" and his power to see that it was executed was clear. Events followed quickly our investigation and recommendations, and I was obliged to ask for the army and navy and by authority of President Roosevelt to institute a provisional government, which lasted nearly two years. It restored order and provided a fair election law, conducted a fair election, and turned that government over to the officers elected under the Constitution of Cuba. There were some mutterings by Senators that under the Platt Amendment, Congress only could decide to take action. However, the matter never reached the adoption of a resolution. Congress appropriated the money needed to meet the extraordinary military and naval expenditures required, and recognized the provisional government in Cuba in such a way as to make the course taken a precedent.

Nor are the laws of the execution of which the President is to take care, confined to express Congressional statutes and provisions having force of law in treaties. The Supreme Court has declared that any obligation inferable from the Constitution, or any duty of the President or the Attorney-General to be derived from the general code of his duties under the laws of the United States is a law within the meaning of this phrase. This was decided in an interesting case from California. Sarah Althea Hill, a resident in California, said she was married to Ex-Senator Sharon of Nevada, and Senator Sharon said she was not. She brought suit in the courts of California to secure a divorce, with alimony, to be satisfied out of his very large estate, and made proof of the marriage by introducing a letter purporting to be written by Senator Sharon admitting the marriage. Senator Sharon then went into the Federal Court as a citizen of Nevada, and sued Miss Hill of California to compel her to deliver up this paper purporting to be a letter of his, on the ground that it was false and forged, and that she was using it to his detriment, as she certainly was. In the Federal Court, Mr. Justice Field rendered several decisions adverse to Miss Hill's claims. Meantime, Senator Sharon had died and Miss Hill had married her counsel, Judge Terry. When Justice Field was delivering one of his judgments, adverse to Mrs. Terry, Judge and Mrs. Terry were in the court-room, and Mrs. Terry rose and denounced Judge Field and attempted to assault him. He sent her to jail for thirty days. He also sent Judge Terry to jail for assault made by him upon the court bailiffs after Mrs. Terry's arrest. Judge and Mrs. Terry then and frequently thereafter threatened that when the opportunity came they would kill Judge Field. The Justice returned to Washington to sit upon the Supreme Court and notice of the threats was brought to the attention of Attorney-General Miller. He deemed them serious enough to direct the United States Marshal of California to assign a deputy to accompany Justice Field when he was traveling upon the circuit the next year in California. This was done. After having held court at Los Angeles, Mr. Justice Field was traveling to San Francisco to hold court there. He got out of the train at Lathrop, a station near Fresno, to breakfast. At the same time a train arrived from San Francisco upon which were Judge and Mrs. Terry. Justice Field had entered the restaurant when the Terrys came in and saw him. Mrs. Terry at once returned to her sleeping car to secure a revolver which she had left in her satchel. Judge Terry advanced toward Judge Field, and as the court found, attacked him from behind. Neagle, the Deputy United States Marshal, who was protecting Judge Field, rose, called to Terry that he was an officer, and demanded that he cease his attack. Terry, as Neagle testified, made a movement as if to draw a weapon, and in defense of Justice Field Neagle shot twice and killed Terry. Neagle was indicted in the state court of California for murder for killing Terry. He applied to the Circuit Court of the United States for a writ of *habeas corpus* to discharge him from the custody of the state court, on the ground that the act for which he had been indicted he had committed in pursuance of a law of the United States, and that under the Federal statute giving in such case the right of release by *habeas corpus* by the Federal Courts he was entitled to his discharge. Judge Sawyer, of the Circuit Court, granted Neagle's application and released him. The state of California carried the case to the Supreme Court of the

United States. The question was whether in the absence of an express statute giving the President or the Attorney-General of the United States or the United States Marshal the duty and power to protect a United States Judge in the discharge of his duties such protection was an act in pursuance of a law of the United States. The Court likened the word "law" to the term "laws" in the constitutional obligation of the President to take care that the laws of the United States be faithfully executed, and Mr. Justice Miller, speaking for the Court, held that the government of the United States, in view of the constitutional provision for the appointment of Judges and the establishment of a system of courts, was under an obligation to protect its Judges from assault by disappointed litigants when those Judges were in the discharge of their official duties, and that such an obligation constituted a law which it was the duty of the President to take care should be faithfully executed. He said, "It would be a great reproach to the system of government of the United States, declared to be within its sphere, sovereign and supreme, if there is to be found within the domain of its powers no means of protecting its Judges in the conscientious and faithful discharge of their duties from malice and hatred of those upon whom their judgments may operate unfavorably."

Speaking of the injunction upon the President to take care that the laws be faithfully executed, he said, "Is this duty limited to the enforcement of acts of Congress or of treaties of the United States according to their express terms, or does it include the rights, duties and obligation growing out of the Constitution itself, our international relations and all the protection implied by the nature of the government under the Constitution?" He affirms the latter alternative.

He then cites the action of a captain of a United States naval vessel in compelling the surrender in the harbor of Smyrna, by an Austrian vessel, of Kotza, a Hungarian, who had made his declaration of intention to become a citizen of the United States, as an instance in which the Executive enforced "a law" of the United States, not on the statute book, in protecting an "embryo" American citizen against foreign aggression. He instances as analogous cases the action of the President in ordering the army and marshals of the United States to maintain the safety of the mails, and to protect public land from trespassers, all in the interest of the government, and all without express statutory authority so to do.

The same principle seems to be exemplified in Logan against the United States, 144 U. S. 263–284. There a band conspired to kill certain prisoners in the custody of a United States Marshal, and being carried from court to a jail. The prisoners were handcuffed and shackled, and several of them as well as their assailants were killed in the attack. The surviving conspirators were indicted under a statute of the United States punishing a conspiracy to injure or oppress any citizen in the free exercise or enjoyment of "a right then and there secured to him by the Constitution of the United States." Neither the Constitution nor any statute expressly provides for protection of a United States prisoner from assault or conspiracy. But the Court held that he does have a right under the Constitution to be protected from assault. Mr. Justice Gray, speaking for the Court, said, "In this case the United States having the absolute right to hold prisoners, have an equal duty to protect them while so held against assault or injury from any quarter. The existence of that duty on the part of the government necessarily implied a corresponding right of the prisoner to be so protected and this right of the prisoners is a right secured to them by the Constitution and laws of the United States."

Let me give another example of a law not embodied in a statute or treaty, which, due to Congressional neglect to act, the President has had to see executed.

By an act approved April 28th, 1904, the President was directed to take possession and occupy on behalf of the United States the Canal Zone, the dominion over which had been acquired under the Hay-Varilla Treaty, just then ratified. The seventh section of the act provided "that all the military, civil and judicial powers, as well as the power to make the rules and regulations necessary for the government of the Canal Zone, should be vested in such a person and should be exercised in such a manner as the President should direct until the expiration of the 58th Congress."

When the 58th Congress expired no further provision had been made for the government of the Zone. I was Secretary of War from 1904 to 1908, and in charge of the Canal work. The question arose as to what was to be done in this legislative lapse of government after the death of the 58th Congress. I had no hesitation in advising the President, and I may add he had no hesitation in accepting the advice, that his statutory duty was to build the Canal, and his constitutional duty to take care that the laws be faithfully executed required him to maintain the existing government and continue the *status quo* which was necessary to the construction of the Canal. Congress made no further provision for the government of the Zone for seven years, and by its acquiescence vindicated this view of the President's duty. It is true that one Congressman, now the Governor General of the Philippines, rose in his place in Congress to denounce our usurpation, but except for his lucubration on the subject, no objection was made in Congress and no action was taken. The truth was that Congress did not know exactly what to do and so left it to the President to assume the responsibility.

The President is the Commander-in-Chief of the army and navy, and the militia when called into the service of the United States. Under this, he can order the army and navy anywhere he will, if the appropriations furnish the means of transportation. Of course the instrumentality which this power furnishes, gives the President an opportunity to do things which involve consequences that it would be quite beyond his power under the Constitution directly to effect. Under the Constitution, only Congress has the power to declare war, but with the army and the navy, the President can take action such as to involve the country in war and to leave Congress no option but to declare it or to recognize its existence. This was the charge made against President Polk in beginning the Mexican War. War as a legal fact, it was decided by the Supreme Court in Prize cases, can exist by invasion of this country by a foreign enemy or by such an insurrection as occurred during the Civil War, without any declaration of war by Congress at all, and it is only in the case of a war of our aggression against a foreign country that the power of Congress must be affirmatively asserted to establish its legal existence.

What constitutes an act of war by the land or naval forces of the United States is sometimes a nice question of law and fact. It really seems to differ with the character of the nation whose relations with the United States are affected. The unstable condition as to law and order of some of the Central American Republics seems to create different rules of international law from those that obtain in governments that can be depended upon to maintain their own peace and order. It has been frequently necessary for the President to direct the landing of naval marines from United States vessels in Central America to protect the American consulate and American citizens and their property. He has done this under his general power as Commander-in-Chief. It grows not out of any specific act of Congress, but out of that obligation, inferable from the Constitution, of the government to protect the rights of an American citizen against foreign aggression, as in the Kotza incident, cited by Mr. Justice Miller in the Neagle case. In practice the use of the naval marines for such a purpose has become so common that their landing is treated as a mere local police measure, whereas if troops of the regular army are used for such a purpose, it seems to take on the color of an act of war.

Thus it would be difficult to explain the landing of our army in Vera Cruz by force, as anything but an act of war to punish the government of Huerta in Mexico for its refusal to render what was deemed by President Wilson as a proper apology for a violation of our international rights in the arrest of some of our sailors. This act was committed before authority was given by Congress, but the necessary authority for it had passed one House and was passing another at the time, and the question as to the right of the Executive to take the action without Congressional authority was avoided by full and immediate ratification.

In Nicaragua in my administration, an insurrection had led to the immurement of American citizens by insurrectos and the threatened destruction of American property. The President of Nicaragua, whom we had recognized and whose Minister we had received, called upon us to protect our own citizens and their property because he was unable to render them the protection which their treaty rights gave them. This led to the landing of marines and quite a campaign, which resulted in the maintenance of law and order and the elimination of the insurrectos. This was not an act of war, because it was done at the request and with the consent of the lawful authorities of the territory where it took place.

As Commander-in-Chief and in taking care that the laws be faithfully executed, President Cleveland sent General Miles to Chicago to remove the obstruction to the passage of the mails and of interstate commerce which Debs at the head of the American Railway Union was effecting by violence and other unlawful means. This was the case where Governor Altgelt sought by protest to keep the army out of Illinois, on the ground that until he or the legislature requested it, the President had no right to send it into the state for the purpose of suppressing disorder. President Cleveland and Attorney-General Olney earned the gratitude of all lovers of peace and good order by the firm stand which they took in this matter and in maintaining what the Supreme Court had so often decided, that every foot of land within the jurisdiction of the United States, whether in a state or territory, or in the District of Columbia, is territory of the United States upon which the laws of the United States can be executed by the President with all the forces which he has at his lawful command ; that there is a peace of the United States, a violation of which consists in forcible resistance to Federal laws. Mr. Cleveland did not have to consult Governor Altgelt as to whether he should send an army to Illinois to see that the peace of the United States was preserved and that the Federal laws were faithfully executed there. The full legality of President Cleveland's action in this regard was sustained by the unanimous judgment of the Supreme Court in the Debs case.

The Constitution provides that the United States shall protect each state against invasion and on the application of the Legislature, or of the Executive when the Legislature cannot be convened, against domestic violence ; and an early statute of the United States, still in force, provides that on such an application the President may use the militia of any state or the regular army to suppress such insurrection. In the case of Rhode Island as between claimants for the governor-ship, the court held that it was within the power of the Federal Executive conclusively to determine so far as that court was concerned who was the governor of the state, a result quite analogous to that which enables the President to recognize foreign governments and to bind all other departments of the government by his recognition.

There is, however, a far wider exercise of the authority by the Executive in his capacity as Commander-in-Chief. It was exemplified in and after the Spanish War. Before and after the Treaty of Paris was made with Spain, by which there were left in our possession, as owners, the Philippines and Porto Rico, and in our custody, as trustees for the people of Cuba, the Island of Cuba, we acquired responsibilities which were met by occupation of those islands and their government by our army and navy. In the case of Cuba, this continued from 1898 until 1903, when the island was turned over to the Cuban Republic. In the case of Porto Rico this continued from 1898 until the taking effect of the Foraker Act in April, 1900, and in the Philippines from August 13th, 1898, when we took Manila, until March, 1902, when the President was expressly given power to establish a civil government there. During all this interval of Congressional silence, and acquiescence in the action of the President as Commander-in-Chief, he directly, or through his appointed agents, exercised all the executive power and all the legislative power of government in those territories. After suppressing actual disorder, he created a quasi-civil government and appointed an executive, a civil legislature and civil judges, and became the lawgiver of ten millions of people for a period ranging from two years to four. There was nothing new or startling in the principle of this temporary enlargement of his executive functions. Its novelty was in the great volume of power which the circumstances thrust on him and the extent of the responsibilities and the wide discretion which he had to exercise. The validity of such action had been recognized by the Supreme Court in similar cases arising after the Mexican War, when we took over California and New Mexico. The delay of Congress was useful in all these cases. In respect to Porto Rico, Congress probably acted too quickly, for the Foraker Act, which provided for its government, was made like the usual territorial acts in the United States, and it did not fit quite the civilization to which it was applied in this community of Spanish laws and customs. In the Philippines, under the wise and statesmanlike foresight of Secretary Root the civil government was framed gradually in that country to suit the exigencies. Congress was quite willing to let President McKinley handle the difficult problems until experience should throw light on the situation. When it did act, it ratified everything the President had done and continued under its authority the government which had been initiated and created by the Commander-in-Chief.

There is an instance of Congressional ratification in which I took part that has some humorous features that perhaps would make it of interest to repeat it.

In 1902, while I was Governor of the Philippines, I returned to this country and visited Washington, and had the pleasure of spending thirty days with Mr. Root as his guest. One Sunday afternoon, while we were talking over Philippine matters, he called my attention to the fact that a question had been raised as to the right of the then Philippine Government, without express Congressional authority, to impose duties on goods imported into the Philippines from the United States. These duties had been a source of a large part of the revenues which we used in carrying on the government in the Islands. He said to me, "Now, Taft, we have collected this money, and we have disbursed it, and if there is any doubt about it, we ought to remove that doubt and not be put in the attitude of unlawfully extorting money and expending it for governmental purposes. Therefore, let's draw up a section for the pending Philippine bill, which shall ratify the collection of these duties." Accordingly, we sat down and jointly drafted such a section which was made a part of the Philippine Act, passed in July, 1902, for the government of the Islands. Thereafter a series of suits were brought to recover back the duties collected by the Philippine Government on goods imported from the United States. The total amount sought to be recovered in these suits was about $3,000,000. One of the suits seeking to recover from the United States $100,000, by Warner, Barnes & Company, was brought to a hearing in the Court of Claims and there defeated, on the ground that there was war in the Philippines and the general commanding had the right to levy duties as he chose. The matter of ratification by Congress was not very much considered. The case was carried to the Supreme Court. The Supreme Court reversed the decision and gave judgment for Warner, Barnes & Company for the full $100,000. The question of ratification was summarily considered by the Court, and to the disgust of Mr. Root and myself, the Court held that the clause which we had drafted for the purpose of ratifying the action of the Philippine Government in collecting these duties, was not intended by Congress to effect the very ratification which we sought. The joke was certainly on us. After the opinion of the Court was announced, the counsel for all these claims, who I am advised was very largely interested in their recovery, because his fee was to be a percentage, came to ask me, then Secretary of War, to consent to an entry of the same judgment in all the other suits, which would have amounted to a judgment for $3,000,000 against the government. I felt very indignant over what I regarded as the injustice and inequity of the decision. These claimants had been able to collect the amount of the duties in the prices at which they sold the goods in the Philippines, and now they were seeking to make the government pay twice to them after it had used the money collected to give them a good government. In a somewhat heated conversation with counsel, I expressed my feelings in regard to the judgment of the Court in such a way as to lead him to denounce me as an anarchist and not properly respectful to the judgment of the highest tribunal in the world. I declined utterly to consent to any judgment and notified him of an intention to file an application for a rehearing. Such an application was filed, and to the surprise of counsel, was granted, because the judgment had been a unanimous judgment and it was supposed that a rehearing would never be granted in such a case. The case was then reargued, and in that hearing the importance of the ratification by Congress was emphasized. We did not succeed in inducing the Court to reverse itself, though we did elicit from the member of the Court writing the opinion that there were some parts of the record that had escaped his attention. Two of the judges dissented from the judgment of the Court. It then occurred to me that if the question turned on ratification, it was not too late to ratify the collections as to all the claims except that one which had passed into judgment. So I went to Mr. Joseph Cannon, the Chairman of the Appropriations Committee of the House, and presented the case to him. I don't think Mr. Cannon has ever done any work more valuable for the government than he did as the watchdog of the Treasury, even though he sometimes had a profane bark. He at once fell in with my suggestion that we have a second clause of ratification which would leave no doubt in the mind of the Court that Congress intended to ratify the collection of the duties in question. I also consulted Mr. Hale, of Maine, who was Chairman of the Committee on Appropriations in the Senate, and enlisted his active coöperation. We had a fight on the floor of the House and the Senate before we succeeded in putting the ratification through. The question then came up again on the second ratification and in that case we secured a majority of the court, Mr. Justice White pronouncing the judgment in favor of the effectiveness of the ratification, and in this way we defeated what I have always regarded as an inequitable claim. Of course those of us who were interested thought that the last judgment was a deliverance of a Daniel come to judgment. I do not say that there is any association between that judgment and the fact that the Judge who pronounced the majority opinion is now the Chief Justice of the United States; but so he is.

CHAPTER V

ONE of the President's most important powers is that which he exercises over our foreign relations. We are just now very much interested in the issues between us and foreign countries. They seem to be dwarfing domestic questions. The greatest war the world ever saw comes close to us. Our attitude as a neutral, and the necessary interference with the commerce between us and belligerents, raises controversies which call for the utmost care in their negotiation and settlement.

It is well to premise what I have to say about the Executive power in such matters by pointing out the exclusive jurisdiction that the Federal government has in dealing with foreign nations. In our domestic matters, the Executive power is divided between the President, the governors of the states, the Legislative power between Congress and the Legislatures of the states, and the Judicial power between the Federal Judiciary and the state courts; but when we come to governmental action with respect to foreign countries, we find that the framers of the Constitution were most careful to vest in the national government complete jurisdiction, and industriously excluded by express prohibition the interference of the states therein. Thus the President and the Senate were given power to make treaties with foreign nations, while all states are expressly forbidden to make them. Congress is given power to regulate foreign commerce, to levy import and tonnage duties, to declare war and to maintain armies and navies for the purpose of carrying on war, to authorize privateers to prey upon the enemy's commerce, to make rules concerning captures on land and water, to make a uniform rule of naturalization, and to denounce and punish offenses against the law of nations, while the states are expressly forbidden to declare war, to grant letters of marque and reprisal, or indeed to maintain a navy or a standing army, or to levy import or tonnage duties. The Federal Courts are given jurisdiction in all cases affecting Ambassadors and other public Ministers and Consuls, and in cases arising between a state or the citizens thereof and foreign states, citizens and subjects; while the President is given the power to appoint Ambassadors, with the advice and consent of the Senate, and to receive Ambassadors from foreign countries, and as Commander-in-Chief of the army and navy to repel invasions and to carry on the war declared by Congress.

The first and most important duty connected with foreign relations that the President has is that of initiating and drafting treaties with foreign nations and submitting them to the Senate for the Senate's advice and consent, and a two-thirds vote of those present is required in the Senate lawfully to advise and consent to a treaty. Originally in the Constitutional Convention, it was proposed that the Senate should appoint Ambassadors and should make treaties; but toward the latter part of the Convention a change was made in this regard, and the power of the President was very much amplified ; and in the matter of treaties it was given to him to negotiate them and to ratify and proclaim them. ,Neither the Senate nor the House, nor both of them together, can compel the President to make a treaty. He has the sole initiative in this regard. Nor is he bound, after he has made a treaty, and the Senate has advised and consented to it, to ratify it and proclaim it, and the treaty does not go into effect until its ratification. There have been many discussions in the Senate over this treaty-making power, and Senators have assumed that the Senate was the more important factor in the making of treaties than the Executive. They have usually in their arguments referred to the fact that Madison moved in the Convention that the Senate should make the treaties without the intervention of the Executive, and that it was at first adopted. But I am not able to discover why this history of the present constitutional provision should exalt the Senate or make more important its existing power. It is the present text of the fundamental law that determines who shall exercise the powers which it confers, and I do not understand why the function that the Senate performs is any more important or any more sacred than that of the Executive in the making of treaties.

This leads me to refer to the ground upon which two-thirds of the Senate refused to advise and consent to the general arbitration treaties negotiated by Secretary Knox during my administration with England and France. The treaties in effect provided that the countries concerned should submit all questions capable

of judicial solution arising between them, which could not
be settled by negotiation, to the decision of an arbitral
tribunal, and in case of a difference, to submit to a
preliminary tribunal the question whether an issue
arising was capable of judicial solution and therefore
must be arbitrated under the treaty. A number of
Senators objected to the effect of these treaties in that
they took away from the Senate the power to withhold
consent to an arbitration of a future issue and thus prevented the Senate from exercising the constitutional
function with which it is charged, of dealing with foreign
relations as they arise. It was argued that such a treaty
would be delegating to the permanent arbitral court a decision as to our foreign relations which was vested in the
Senate, and that it was unconstitutional for the Senate to
consent to make such a delegation. This view it seems
to me is radically wrong, or else it proves too much.
There is no difference in principle between the consent
of the Senate that an existing issue between us and a
foreign nation shall be settled by arbitration and an
agreement that future questions of a defined class shall
be so settled. If the submission of a question to arbitration is a delegation to the arbitration tribunal of the
power vested in the Senate over our foreign relations,
then the Senate has no power to consent to arbitration
at all; and yet this it has done since the foundation of
the government. But it is said that by delegating to a
preliminary tribunal the question whether the issue
arising is within the terms of the treaty or not, the
Senate is delegating its power. This view is as faulty
as the other one. The question whether an issue is
arbitrable within the classification of the treaty is a

question of the construction of a treaty ; and one of the commonest subjects of arbitration is the proper construction of a treaty. Therefore, if the Senate were to consent to abide the judgment of a tribunal in the future as to whether an issue arising between us and a foreign nation is within a class of arbitrable questions described in a treaty, it is only consenting to arbitrate the construction of the treaty when the event occurs which requires construction. This it has done in numerous treaties already.

The Senate is therefore wrong in its view of this matter, if its view is to rest on the limitations of its constitutional powers. If its view rests merely on the question of expediency, that is a different thing, and I do not need to argue that. But I think it is of the utmost importance that every one interested in the establishment of a League of Nations, for the settlement of differences between them by an international court, should realize that the attitude of the Senate upon the point I have been discussing would make it impossible for the United States to become a member of such a League. I am anxious, therefore, in season and out of season, to argue as forcibly as I may the error of the Senate in this regard.

The treaty-making power is a very broad one. Indeed, it is much more important under our Constitution than in any other country that I know. According to our Constitution, a treaty of the United States, in so far as its provisions are in an appropriate form to operate as such, is a law in the United States, exactly as a statute of Congress is a law in the United States. I think I have already invited your attention to the fact that a treaty may repeal a law of Congress if it is inconsistent with it, and that a law of Congress may repeal a treaty. A treaty operates both as a binding contract with a foreign nation and as municipal law. As a contract binding upon both parties, it cannot be made to lose its obligation by a refusal of either country to perform it. It is thus broken, but the party injured by the breach has in international law a right to damages from the party breaking it. If Congress passes a statute inconsistent with the treaty, while it breaks the treaty it repeals it as municipal law. It does not relieve the nation from its moral and international obligation to make good the breach by damages or otherwise, but it does change the law which binds the officers, citizens and others within the governmental jurisdiction of the United States, to comply not with the treaty, but with the law which abrogated it. This was the effect of the decision of the Supreme Court in the Chinese cases. Under our treaty with China certain classes of Chinese were entitled to come into the country. Congress desired to exclude many of the classes thus entitled, and passed a law doing so. The law broke the treaty, but the immigration officers, the courts and all persons within the territorial jurisdiction of the United States were obliged to conform to the act of Congress, and to exclude those Chinese who had the right to come in under the treaty but were forbidden to do so by the subsequent law.

The treaty-making power is in some respects wider than the power of Congress in the enactment of statutes, in this: As between the states and the Federal government, Congressional legislation is limited to a Federal field marked by the powers expressly granted to Congress within the Constitution and those which may be reasonably implied as necessary and proper to the exercise of the express powers. All other powers are exercised by the legislatures of the state within the restrictions of their respective Constitutions. The treaty-making power, however, is dealing with our foreign relations, and when we deal with our foreign relations, we are a nation undivided and presenting a united front. Everything, therefore, that is natural or customarily involved in such foreign relations, a treaty may cover, whether beyond the law-making power of Congress and within the control of state legislatures, or not. Now one of the usual subjects for consideration of a treaty is the rights of the citizens or subjects of one country while resident in, or passing through, the country of the other, to security of life and limb, to the carrying on of business, or to the inheriting of property or its transmission. The subjects of regulating business in a state, the inheritance of property and its transmission are ordinarily within the cognizance of state legislatures and are not within the power of Congress. Yet by a treaty, aliens may be given rights in a state in respect to such matters even though this is at variance with the laws of the state, and to that extent the treaty-making power controls the statute of the state. It makes an exception to the state statute, in favor of the aliens whose rights are defined in the treaty. This has been decided so many times that there is no doubt about the correctness of the view. The Supreme Court has declined to imply the same limitations upon the treaty-making power as the Constitution imposes upon Congressional law-making. It has said that the treaty-making power would not of course reach to changing a form of state government or perhaps parting with state territory, but it has left quite general and undefined the field that it may occupy.

Sometimes the Executive has not made a treaty with a foreign government, but has recommended to Congress the passage of a law, which, with similar action by the other country, constitutes an agreement between them. Thus the statute authorizing reciprocity with Canada, which passed Congress during my administration, relating to the imposition of duties in this country, which was to take effect upon the enactment of a corresponding law in Canada, would, if Canada had passed a similar statute, have constituted an agreement from which each government could withdraw at will. It was not in form a contract or a treaty. So, too, when I was Secretary of War, President Roosevelt sent me to Panama to adjust the relations between the United States and Panama under the Hay-Varilla Treaty. That treaty was very hastily drawn, and many things were left most indefinite, as for instance the boundaries of the Zone at the termini of the Zone. The Zone was not to include the town of Colon or the town of Panama and yet there was no official delimitation in the records of Panama or Colombia of either town. We were to occupy the same bed with the Panamanians, but our half was in the middle. This created in many ways an embarrassing situation, and in some way or other a *modus vivendi* had to be established. The absence of it had caused great irritation and threatened to obstruct the carrying on of the construction of the Canal. I agreed with the President of the Republic upon a plan by which we might comfortably and peaceably take and occupy our half and the people and government of Panama might keep on either side. The plan contained a great many different provisions. I had no power to make a treaty with Panama, but I did have, with the authority of the President, the right to make rules equivalent to law in the Zone. I therefore issued an order directing the carrying out of the plan agreed upon in so far as it was necessary to carry it out on our side of the line, on condition that, and as long as, the regulations to be made by Panama were enforced by that government. This was approved by Secretary Hay and the President and has constituted down until the present day, I believe, the basis upon which the two governments are carried on in this close proximity. It was attacked vigorously in the Senate as a usurpation of the treaty-making power, and I was summoned before a committee in the Senate to justify what had been done. There was a great deal of eloquence over this usurpation of the Senate's prerogative by Mr. Morgan and other Senators, but the *modus vivendi* continued as the practical agreement between the nations for certainly more than seven years, and my impression is that it is still in force in most of its provisions.

The President has a very large authority outside of treaty-making in our foreign relations. He appoints our Ambassadors to other countries, and he receives Ambassadors from them. This gives him necessarily the duty of carrying on foreign negotiations between ourselves and foreign countries. He and he alone is the representative of our nation in dealing with foreign nations. When I say he alone, I mean that it is he to whom the foreign nations look. He has Ambassadors and Ministers and Consuls in other countries, but they only represent him. In receiving foreign Ambassadors and in sending them, he is bound to determine, when there is any dispute, who the lawful government is, to whom he wishes to accredit his Ambassador and from whom he wishes to receive an Ambassador. Therefore in him is necessarily vested the power and duty of recognizing the lawful government of any country. The influence that he can exert in his recognition of a foreign government we have seen illustrated in President Wilson's refusal to recognize Huerta and his announcement that he never would recognize him. We can see the same influence at work at present in behalf of Carranza, whom he has recognized as the *de facto* President against Villa.

The President carries on the correspondence through the State Department with all foreign countries. He is bound in such correspondence to discuss the proper construction of treaties. He must formulate the foreign policies of our government. He must state our attitude upon questions constantly arising. While strictly he may not bind our government as a treaty would bind it, to a definition of its rights, still in future discussions foreign Secretaries of other countries are wont to look for support of their contentions to the declarations and admissions of our Secretaries of State in other controversies as in a sense binding upon us. There is thus much practical framing of our foreign policies in the executive conduct of our foreign relations.

One of the most important strokes in our international history was the correspondence carried on by Secretary Hay under President McKinley in the establishment of the policy of the open door in China and equal facilities for all nations in dealing with that important empire. That policy was stated in a note by Secretary Hay and acquiesced in by all the nations concerned, and that without any advice and consent of the Senate.

Whenever our American citizens have claims to present against a foreign nation, they do it through the President by the State Department; and when foreign citizens have claims to present against us, they present them through their diplomatic representatives to our State Department, and the formulation and the discussion of the merits of those claims create an important body of precedents in our foreign policy.

The importance of the President in our foreign relations, when his power in that regard is considered in connection with his duty to take care that the laws are faithfully executed, and with his duty as Commander-in-Chief to direct the movements of the Army and Navy, may be noted in the authority which President McKinley exercised to take part in the so-called "Boxer War," in China. The lawless uprising in that ancient Empire against foreigners, which for the time being overthrew the power of the Imperial Government, exposed to danger the lives of the diplomatic representatives of foreign nations at Pekin, and brought about the murder of one of them. Uniting with other governments, President McKinley, without

express Congressional authority, ordered the land and
naval forces of the United States into a campaign to
rescue the foreign legations which were besieged in
Pekin.

There has always been a dispute as to whether the
treaty-making power can bind Congress to the obligation of a treaty, so that if a treaty provides for the
payment of money, Congress is under an obligation
to appropriate the money.   Of course a treaty may not
take money out of the Treasury of the United States,
because under the Constitution that can only be taken
out by Congress, but it has always seemed to me that
while Congress in appropriating money for any purpose
exercises its discretion, in that it has the actual power
to pay or not to pay, it is bound in honor to perform
the contract which the government of the United States
has made through that agency appointed by the Constitution to make the contract.   When Congress in its
discretion, as the appropriating branch of the government, refuses to appropriate the money which the
treaty-making power has agreed shall be paid it is
merely violating the plighted faith of the government.
Just so, it may abrogate a treaty obligation by statute,
but it does not annul the obligation.   It is exercising
the same power that a man has to refuse to pay his
note after he has made it through an authorized agent.
The man can be compelled to pay his note.   Congress
may not be compelled because of its exercising the
functions of sovereignty, but its failure to act does not
destroy its obligation.

The President may not annul or abrogate a treaty
without the consent of the Senate unless he is given

that specific authority by the terms of the treaty. The
ending of a treaty is to be effected by the same power
which made the treaty. An instance in my own experience of annulling a treaty comes to me. We had a
treaty with Russia proclaimed in 1832. It was a treaty
of commerce and friendship. It gave to our merchants
certain rights in Russia in carrying on business. Russia
refused to extend the rights assured to our merchants to
Jews, on the ground that Jews in Russia were limited
in their commercial activities and were obliged to carry
them on within a pale in that country, and that when
our merchants being Jews sought to avail themselves of
the privileges of the treaty, they were either denied
admission or were subjected to the local laws of Russia
and were limited as their coreligionists were limited in
Russia. From the time that the question was mooted
the two countries had differed as to construction. A
similar question had arisen between France and Russia
and between England and Russia, but Russia had
always insisted upon maintaining the position I have
described. The attitude so contrary to our notions of
equity and tolerance to all religions naturally irritated
our people and led to the introduction of a resolution
in the House of Representatives, during my administration, calling upon the President to annul the treaty
in accordance with its terms by a year's notice, on the
ground that Russia had flagrantly violated its obligations. The resolution was drawn in language which
would have given diplomatic offense to Russia, as
doubtless its framers intended to do. With the responsibility of maintaining as friendly relations as possible with all the world, it seemed to me that if the

treaty had to be abrogated, it ought to be done as politely as possible, with the hope of negotiating a treaty less subject to dispute, and giving more satisfactory result. With the knowledge that the resolution was sure to pass the Senate, I took the step of annulling the treaty myself and giving a year's notice to Russia of the annulment in proper and courteous expressions, on the ground that we had differed so radically as to its construction and the treaty was so old that it would be wiser to make a new treaty more definite and satisfactory. I sent notice of this annulment at once to the Senate, and in this way succeeded in having the Senate substitute a resolution approving my action for the resolution which came over from the House. The House was thus induced to approve my action and the incident was closed for the time. I regret to say that no new treaty has yet been made and our relations with Russia in many regards are defined only by the rules of international law.

The Supreme Court recognizes the power of the President to decide the question of our foreign relations which it calls political, and holds itself bound by the President's action. Early in our history the question arose whether the Falkland Islands belonged to Buenos Aires, so that Buenos Aires might pass a law punishing the killing of seals in those Islands. Our State Department, in correspondence with the government of Buenos Aires, had refused to recognize its lawful jurisdiction there. In a maritime insurance case, the issue was whether a vessel lost through seizure by the authorities of Buenos Aires for violation of its sealing laws was a loss within a marine insurance policy, or was excepted because the master had violated the statutes of a lawful government. The Supreme Court held that it would follow the decision of the President as the political department having the authority to decide such an issue. The Court reached a similar conclusion in another seal case where we were on the other side. Mr. Blaine, as Secretary of State for Mr. Harrison, had claimed in a correspondence with Lord Salisbury that through the grant of Alaska and the adjoining waters we were given jurisdiction over the open Bering Sea to arrest Canadian sealers engaged in pelagic sealing contrary to the laws of the United States. Mr. Blaine's claim was that Russia had asserted territorial jurisdiction over these waters, and that this jurisdiction had been acquiesced in by the world. The Supreme Court intimated in its opinion that this was a political question, and that it would not undertake to discuss the merits of Mr. Blaine's contentions, because it was bound to follow and respect the attitude of the President and Secretary of State in deciding such a question. Of course the decision of Congress or the treaty making power upon such an issue would be binding upon the Courts, but in the absence of the decision of either the action of the President is conclusive with the Courts.

The last power of the President which I shall consider is the power of pardon. This is a wide power, and enables the President to pardon any one guilty of an offense against the United States before indictment, after indictment and before conviction, or after conviction. He need not name the persons to be pardoned if he pardons a class and makes provision by which the persons affected shall establish their membership in that class. The pardon under such circumstances is called an amnesty. He is expressly given power to grant reprieves, which means only a suspension of the execution of a sentence for one purpose or another. The Supreme Court said in one case that a pardon reaches both the punishment prescribed for the offense and the guilt of the offender, and when the pardon is full, it relieves the punishment and blots out of existence the guilt, so that in the eye of the law the offender is as innocent as if he never had committed the offense. This is rather a strong statement as some later cases show. It is difficult to clothe Omnipotence with such a power.

Congress may not restrict the President in the exercise of his power of pardon. There was a good deal of conflict between the Executive and Congress in respect to amnesty proclamations issued by President Johnson. Congress was loath to allow the full constitutional effect which such pardons required in respect to the status of those who had been guilty of treason against the government and who were restored to the enjoyment of their full civil rights, as if the treason had never been committed. In the case of Mr. Garland, who was afterwards a Senator from Arkansas, and Attorney-General of the United States, the Supreme Court had to examine the validity of a statute, which required that every attorney practising law in the Federal court must take an oath that he never had borne arms against the United States. This act practically excluded all lawyers who had served the Confederacy from the pursuit of their profession. The Court held the act invalid because it was in effect a bill of attainder, and also because it defeated the President's amnesty of which Mr. Garland had taken advantage. A very nice line of distinction is presented by another decision of the Supreme Court, in which the validity of a law of the state of New York was in question. The law prevented men who had been convicted of felonies from receiving certificates permitting them to practise medicine. In that case, the Court held that the question of fitness was one of fact and that the legislature had the right to make rules of eligibility to protect the public against immorality in the practice of the profession, and that it could not say that such a rule of ineligibility was not reasonable in preserving a proper moral standard in physicians. It could not regard it as additional punishment.

There is a question whether the President's power of pardons extends to the case of one sentenced to imprisonment for contempt by a Federal Court. It is objected that this power of contempt is used by the court to enforce its judgments, and that if the President could intervene and paralyze the instrument in the hands of the Court to enforce its judgment, he would not be pardoning a crime but would be obstructing the Court in its administration of justice. I think it is possible to smooth out this difficulty by pointing out a distinction between the two ways in which a court exercises its power of contempt. Where a court is seeking to enforce a decree or a judgment against a contumacious party and puts him in prison for the purpose of compelling him to comply with the judgment or decree, then I do not think the President could pardon a man or relieve him from the effect of such an order because he would really be obstructing the cause of justice. But where the court is merely vindicating its own authority by punishing a man for a past contempt, and where an imprisonment is not a continuing duress for the purpose of compelling obedience, it seems to me that the punishment inflicted is for an offense against the United States, to wit, a defiance of its judicial authority, and therefore that it does come within the range of the power of pardon by the President.

The duty involved in the pardoning power is a most difficult one to perform, because it is so completely within the discretion of the Executive and is lacking so in rules or limitations of its exercise.   The only rule he can follow is that he shall not exercise it against the public interest.   The guilt of the man with whose case he is dealing is usually admitted, and even if it is not, the judgment of the court settles that fact in all but few cases.   The question which the President has to decide is whether under peculiar circumstances of hardship he can exercise clemency without destroying the useful effect of punishment in deterring others from committing crimes.   The frequent result of human punishment is that those near to the criminal or dependent upon him suffer more than he does, and their pitiable condition often furnishes a plea for mitigation of the penalty to the offender.   Those who plead for pardon are generally entirely blind to the right of society to be protected from criminals and to have those of criminal tendencies deterred from yielding to them by fear of punishment. If the fear of punishment is lessened by Executive clemency to those convicted, the benefit of punishment · will be largely lost.   It is a case where organized emotion and sentiment are likely to mislead, to the public detriment. It seems to me that the people of New York and of the country generally are in danger of being led by an unwise sentiment into a treatment of convicted criminals that will neither impart to the criminals the proper lesson from punishment, nor will keep before those likely to become criminals the fear of the law as a deterrent. It is of course wise and humane that state prisons and penitentiaries should be made as healthful as possible for the confinement of those sentenced to spend a term within their walls, and it is wise to provide healthful labor and primary and industrial education. The impulse of many prison reformers, however, to treat the prisoners as victims and to make society the scapegoat for all their sins and vicious propensities and crimes is a wrong one, which if yielded to will certainly lead to bad results and ultimately to a retracing of steps toward greater rigidity and severity. The theory that by treating criminals as if they had no criminal tendencies you can eliminate such tendencies is one that may work in some cases, but the exceptions will be so many as to make the policy ultimately ridiculous, and, worse than ridiculous, most harmful. A man who violates the law in such a way as to call for a sentence and imprisonment is punished for his violation, and he ought to be punished. He need not be, and ought not to be, subjected to cruel or unwholesome surroundings, but he should be made to feel that he is suffering punishment for that which he has done. He may be given an opportunity to reform, and, so far as it is possible, be encouraged to change his ways, but if he is to be coddled and to receive the impression that he is a victim instead of being a criminal, the enforcement of our criminal law will be a failure.

The President has to keep these distinctions in mind in the exercise of Executive clemency, and must stifle his emotions of pity for the family and dependents of the criminal in the consideration of the character of the offense and the necessity for having it plainly understood that such an offender is not to escape with immunity.

There has been a custom in the Presidential office of pardoning men who are supposed to be near their death to enable them to go home and die with their families. The difficulty in such cases is in being certain that death is near. I had two notable cases in which I was assured by the prison authorities that death was imminent, and that if they were to be released at all, to die, they ought to be released at once. I instituted as thorough an investigation as I could through the army and navy surgeons in the employ of the government and reached the conclusion from the evidence submitted that death was certain. I pardoned them both. One man died and kept his contract. The other recovered at once, and seems to be as healthy and active as any one I know. I had a suspicion of fraud in the latter case and instituted an investigation to see whether I had been deceived by the friends of the prisoner or the prisoner himself. I was not able to find the evidence of such fraud.

It has been suggested to me that if the man had been guilty of fraud in inducing me to pardon him, I might have set aside the pardon as void and directed the arrest of the former convict. I do not think that in such a case a pardon could be set aside. I do not think either I or a court would have had the authority to issue a warrant for the arrest of the man and to restore him to prison. It seems to me it would be like a case of a man acquitted by a jury which was bribed by him. He might be thereafter convicted of bribery, but he could not be convicted of the crime of which the verdict of the jury acquitted him.

There are curious notions about pardons in the minds of some people. When Mr. Knox was Attorney-General, a Congressman came to him and said that he would like to have a man pardoned who had been sent to the penitentiary for robbing a post office. He said that the convict had been a great supporter of his and he would like to get him out. Mr. Knox asked him what the ground for pardon was, and he said he was a good fellow and had been his friend. Knox said that was no reason. "But," said the Congressman, "I understand that each Congressman has a right to two pardons during his term and I want this to be one of mine."

CHAPTER VI

THE LIMITATIONS OF THE PRESIDENT'S POWERS

I HAVE considered, at possibly too great length, the chief powers of the Executive under the Federal Constitution. In theory, the Executive power and the Legislative power are independent and separate, but it is not always easy to draw the line and to say where Legislative control and direction to the Executive must cease, and where his independent discretion begins. In theory, all the Executive officers appointed by the President directly or indirectly are his subordinates, and yet Congress can undoubtedly pass laws definitely limiting their discretion and commanding a certain course by them which it is not within the power of the Executive to vary. Fixing the method in which Executive power shall be exercised is perhaps one of the chief functions of Congress. Indeed, by its legislation, it often creates a duty in the Executive which did not before exist. Then in prescribing how that duty is to be carried out, it imposes restrictions that the Executive is bound to observe.

Congress may repose discretion in appointees of the President, which the President may not himself control. The instance I have already given is one of these, in which the Comptroller of the Treasury has independent quasi-judicial authority to pass on the question of what warrants are authorized by appropriation acts to be drawn by him on the funds of the Treasury.

The President can appoint him and remove him, but he may not control him in his construction of appropriation acts and his signing, or withholding his signature from warrants in accordance with that construction.

So, too, as between a court directing the action of a marshal and a contrary order of the President, the marshal is bound by law to follow the court's direction. Indeed, the court may compel him to do so by punishing him for contempt if he refuses to obey the order. If the marshal is obstructed in the performance of his duty, however, and he or the court calls upon the President to send the army to overcome the obstruction, the President cannot be compelled to act.

Two principles, limiting Congressional interference with the Executive powers, are clear. *First*, Congress may not exercise any of the powers vested in the President, and *second*, it may not prevent or obstruct the use of means given him by the Constitution for the exercise of those powers.

In the matter of appointments, Presidents have been quick to resent encroachments by Congress. The power of appointment is not in Congress. In the case of Fitz John Porter, President Arthur made a precedent which prevails. Porter had been sentenced by court-martial for his alleged misconduct in failing to support Pope in the second battle of Bull Run. Twenty years after the court-martial, when Porter's friends were in the majority of Congress, they passed an act authorizing the President to appoint Porter a colonel in the regular army, and to place him on the retired list. President Arthur vetoed the bill, and one of the grounds he gave was that it was an encroachment on the Executive power to make the creation of an office conditioned on the appointment of a named individual. When General Grant was dying at Mt. McGregor, Congress, in response to a throb of sympathy and gratitude throughout the nation, wished to have him put on the retired list as a full general, but when the act was drafted and passed, it did not mention General Grant's name. It merely provided that from among the living Commanding Generals, the President might nominate one, and with the consent of the Senate appoint him to be a general on the retired list, with full pay. The act was passed, General Grant was appointed and confirmed to be a general, with full salary, and the last three months of his life were cheered by this evidence of the continued gratitude of his countrymen.

While Congress may not exercise the power of appointment, it may certainly impose rules of eligibility within which appointees are to be selected. The extent of the right of the President to make appointments, without Congressional control or limitation, has been very recently mooted. An army officer, who was under the statute regulating promotion in the army entitled to a promotion to a vacancy, was not a man whom the President thought ought to be promoted, although he was not subject to removal by a court-martial. He therefore passed him over and nominated the next officer in rank to the vacancy. The then Attorney-General rendered an opinion that the President could not be limited in his appointment of army officers by rules as to promotion in the army contained in the army organization act. I am not aware of what action the Senate has taken. Attempt was made by some proceeding in court to prevent the passing over the officer first entitled, but the jurisdiction of the court to control the Executive evidently could not be maintained. If Congress may not provide by law a rule of eligibility for promotion in the army or navy, or if the President may refuse to conform to such a law, it is difficult to see how Congress can exercise the power which it is given by the Constitution to raise and support armies and make rules for the government and regulation of the land and naval forces. Rules of eligibility for promotion would seem to be rules for the regulation of army forces. No court and no other authority, however, can compel the President to make a nomination, and the only method of preventing his appointing someone other than the one specified by law is for the Senate to refuse to confirm him, or for Congress to withhold an appropriation of his salary, or for the Comptroller of the Treasury to decline to draw a warrant for his salary on the ground of his ineligibility under the law. The question of his salary then might be referred to the Court of Claims through a suit by him, and in that way the judgment of the Court might be invoked upon the validity of the appointment. This, however, is one of the numerous instances in which for practical purposes the Constitution is finally construed by the President and the Senate.

The President is made Commander-in-Chief of the army and navy by the Constitution evidently for the purpose of enabling him to defend the country against invasion, to suppress insurrection and to take care that the laws be faithfully executed. If Congress were to attempt to prevent his use of the army for any of these purposes, the action would be void. During the existence of the Federal election laws, there was a provision enacted by Congress forbidding marshals to call upon the army as a *posse comitatus* to assist them in the enforcement of the election laws, but that was not interfering with the President's power as Commander-in-Chief.   Under another section of the statute, the President has the power to call upon the army, after proclamation, to resist forcible obstruction of any Federal laws.   In other words, he is to maintain the peace of the United States.   I think he would have this power under the Constitution even if Congress had not given him express authority to this end.   Again, in the carrying on of war as Commander-in-Chief, it is he who is to determine the movements of the army and of the navy.   Congress could not take away from him that discretion and place it beyond his control in any of his subordinates, nor could they themselves, as the people of Athens attempted to, carry on campaigns by votes in the market-place.

The President is required by the Constitution from time to time to give to Congress information on the state of the Union, and to recommend for its consideration such measures as he shall judge necessary and expedient, but this does not enable Congress or either House of Congress to elicit from him confidential information which he has acquired for the purpose of enabling him to discharge his constitutional duties, if he does not deem the disclosure of such information prudent or in the public interest.   In the controversy between Washington and Congress, over the performance of the Jay Treaty by payment of money, Congress attempted to secure from Washington the correspondence had between him and Chief Justice Jay, and other correspondence about the treaty on the files of the State Department. Washington maintained that the House of Representatives, which was seeking the information, was not part of the treaty-making power and therefore had no right to secure from him confidential information in respect to the making of the treaty which he did not deem wise to make public. He therefore declined to furnish the correspondence, although the House of Representatives adopted resolutions to protest against his action. The House did, however, appropriate the money stipulated for in the treaty.

In the last days of Grant's administration, when the House was Democratic, and when President Grant was being criticized for spending some of the hot months at Long Branch, the House of Representatives sent him a resolution asking for information as to how many Executive acts were performed at other places than the seat of government. The inquiry evidently aroused the General, for his declination to furnish the information is quite spirited. He declined to admit that under the Constitution he was obliged to perform official acts at the seat of government, and proceeded to show by historical reference that many such acts by former Presidents had been performed at other places in the United States. He filed a statement of the time spent at the seat of government by each President, from which it appeared that the President who was most often absent from Washington and the seat of government was Thomas Jefferson, a full quarter of whose time was spent at Monticello. This seemed a very complete answer to the Democratic majority of the House which in passing the resolution were seeking to make political capital, for they could hardly criticize General Grant for doing that which Mr. Jefferson, the founder of the Democratic Party, had done with even more freedom. A visit to his beautiful country seat at Monticello and a knowledge of the very uncomfortable quarters that he had at the White House in the beginnings of our national capital, may explain why Jefferson went to Monticello whenever he could get away from Washington. More than this, he was a great letter writer, and he could write letters as well from Monticello as he could from the White House. I am glad to say that a more reasonable view is now taken of the right of the President to enjoy a vacation at the seashore or in the mountains, whenever he can be spared from Washington, and it is most satisfactory to those of us who have enjoyed some relief of this kind to know that we have Jefferson's conduct to justify us.

Mr. Jefferson set another example which has constituted a precedent never departed from. In the trial of Aaron Burr for treason, Chief Justice Marshall presided in Richmond, and at the instance of the parties to the suit, he directed a subpœna *duces tecum* to be served on President Jefferson, requiring him to bring with him papers supposed to bear on the issue. Mr. Jefferson wrote a letter to the District Attorney declining to respond to the subpœna, and gave as his reason for doing so that he could not be detained as a witness in a case, because it would interfere with his public duties. To this Chief Justice Marshall responded that apparently all his time was not taken up with governmental duties, which Mr. Jefferson construed to mean a reference to the fact that he spent a great deal of his time at Monticello, and an intimation that he might just as well come to Richmond and testify as to go to Monticello and enjoy his leisure. Mr. Jefferson resented the intimation with all the emphasis and vehemence that Chief Justice Marshall's rulings in political and personal matters usually evoked. No other President, so far as I know, has been subpœnaed to appear in court during his term. General Grant did testify in the criminal case brought against Mr. Babcock, his Secretary, in behalf of the defendant. The deposition was given in the White House and was taken before Chief Justice Waite, and in the presence of the Attorney-General.

The Supreme Court seems to make a broad distinction between issuing process against the President and against his subordinates under laws requiring the specific performance of a definite act. I cannot think that the Court would ever issue a mandamus to compel the President to perform even an act purely ministerial, though it has often issued such a writ against one of his subordinates. The Supreme Court has a number of times intimated that the President's office is of such a high character, that officially he is beyond the compulsory processes of the Court. Thus in the case of Mississippi against Johnson, where it was sought by the state of Mississippi to enjoin President Johnson from carrying out the reconstruction acts, on the ground that they were unconstitutional, the Court refused to issue the writ on two grounds, first that it did not have the power to enforce a writ of injunction against the President, who might decline to obey its writ, and second on the ground that the unconstitutionality of such an act directing an executive officer with respect to the government of a state was a political question which it could not control, but which must be decided by the executive to whose discretion the enforcement of the act was entrusted.

As already said, the court has always fully conceded its duty to recognize, as binding upon it, the political powers exercised by the Executive and Legislative departments of the government under the Constitution. It is not always easy to say what is a political issue. Possibly the latest case of this kind is the one in which a corporation sought to evade the payment of taxes in Oregon, on the ground that the law under which they were exacted had been passed by an initiative and a referendum. It was contended that an initiative and referendum were inconsistent with a republican form of government as understood by the framers of the Constitution, and as the United States guaranteed to each state a republican form of government, such a method of legislation must be invalid and no taxes could be collected under it. The Supreme Court answered that the question whether a state had a republican form of government was a political question for Congress to settle, and that as long as Congress continued to recognize Oregon as a state, it was not for the Court to investigate the question. I think myself that there is no doubt that the term "republican" in that clause in the Constitution was intended to distinguish our kind of government from a monarchical form, and that it was not intended to make a distinction between what is called a republican form of government and a purely democratic or direct form of popular government. Congress is the authority to decide this question, and it has already so decided it in the cases of Oklahoma, of Arizona, and of New Mexico, because the constitutions of those states containing provisions for the initiative and the referendum were before it and were approved.

An instance of how the Legislative and Executive departments can decide a constitutional question without the intervention of Congress may be seen in the appropriation made by one Congress during the Spanish-American War of $3,000,000, to be expended through the War Department with the approval of the President for contingencies that could not be foreseen. This fund was not completely expended for some four or five years after the appropriation. It was a very useful fund, as I can testify, because it enabled us in the administration of the Philippines to meet extraordinary expenses which had to be incurred in the suppression of the insurrection, in the detection of sedition, in the encouragement of friendly relations with the people and in many other ways. The point was made by one member of the appropriation committee that this was an appropriation in support of the army, and therefore must be limited by the Constitution to two years, but the view of the department and of the Comptroller of the Treasury was that this appropriation was not included within the limitation because

it was not for the support of the army and was not
used therefor, although included in the Army Appropriation Bill expended by the War Department in the
suppression of the disorders in the Philippines and in
Cuba.

Executive power is sometimes created by custom,
and so strong is the influence of custom that it seems
almost to amend the Constitution. Take the case of
Postal Treaties. The Constitution says that treaties
with foreign governments shall be made by the President, by and with the advice of a two-thirds vote of
the Senate; and yet postal arrangements in the nature
of treaties had been made between this country and
the European countries before the Constitution was
adopted, and continued to be made after its adoption,
without Senate action, until 1844 when the one postal
treaty that was ever made in that way was signed by
the President and consented to by the Senate. Almost
immediately thereafter Congress passed an act which
authorized the Postmaster-General to make treaties
affecting postal matters, with postal authorities of
other countries, subject to the consent of the President,
and this is an exception grafted on to the Constitution
merely through Executive practice. A similar case is
that of the remission of penalties incurred by steamers
violating the navigation laws. Since the beginning of
the government, the Secretary of the Treasury has
exercised the power to remit these penalties in proper
cases. The pardoning power is given by the Constitution to the President, yet the practice of one hundred
years was recognized by the Supreme Court and it was
held to be valid.

In a very recent case, in which President Roosevelt had exercised the power to withdraw lands, which were open for settlement under an act of Congress, from the operation of the act, and in which course I had followed him with very considerable doubt as to my power, the validity of our action was brought before the Supreme Court and sustained, on the ground that the practice of the Executive for a great many years, with the acquiescence of Congress in such withdrawals, justified the exercise of the power and made it legal as if there had been an express act of Congress authorizing it.

One of the great questions that the Executive has had to meet in the past has been how far he might properly differ from the Supreme Court in the construction of the Constitution in the discharge of his duties. Jefferson, in a letter to Mrs. John Adams, laid it down with emphasis with reference to the Sedition Law, in which he said :

The Judges, believing the law constitutional, had a right to pass a sentence of fine and imprisonment, because the power was placed in their hands by the Constitution. But the executive, believing the law to be unconstitutional, might remit the execution of it, because that power has been confided to them by the Constitution. That instrument meant that its coördinate branches should be checks on each other. But the opinion which gives to the Judges the right to decide what laws are constitutional, and what not, not only for themselves in their own sphere of action, but for the legislature and executive also, in their spheres, would make the judiciary a despotic branch.

And so Jackson in his message vetoing the renewal of the charter to the bank of the United States in respect to the opinion of the Supreme Court confirming the constitutionality of the previous charter, said :

If the opinion of the Supreme Court covered the whole ground of this act, it ought not to control the coördinate authorities of this Government. The Congress, the Executive and the Court must each for itself be guided by its own opinion of the Constitution. Each public officer who takes an oath to support the Constitution swears that he will support it as he understands it, and not as it is understood by others. It is as much the duty of the House of Representatives, of the Senate, and of the President to decide upon the Constitutionality of any bill or resolution which may be presented to them for passage or approval as it is of the Supreme judges when it may be brought before them for judicial decision. The opinion of the judges has no more authority over Congress than the opinion of Congress has over the judges, and on that point the President is independent of both. The authority of the Supreme Court must not, therefore, be permitted to control the Congress or the Executive when acting in their legislative capacities, but to have only such influence as the force of their reasoning may deserve.

Mr. Lincoln in his reference to the Dred Scott case said :

I do not forget the position assumed by some that constitutional questions are to be decided by the Supreme Court, nor do I deny that such decisions must be binding in any case upon the parties to a suit as to the object of that suit, while they are also entitled to very high respect and consideration in all parallel cases by all other departments of the Government. And while it is obviously possible that such decision may be erroneous in any given case, still the evil effect following it, being limited to that particular case, with the chance that it may be overruled and never become a precedent for other cases, can better be borne than could the evils of a different practice. At the same time, the candid citizen must confess that if the policy of the Government upon vital questions affecting the whole people is to be irrevocably fixed by decisions of the Supreme Court, the instant they are made in ordinary litigation between parties in personal actions the people will have ceased to be their own rulers, having to that extent practically resigned

their government into hands of that eminent tribunal. Nor is
there in this view any assault upon the court or the judges. It is a
duty from which they may not shrink to decide cases properly
brought before them, and it is no fault of theirs if others seek to
turn their decisions to political purposes.

I do not intend to dispute the attitude of these distinguished men. Nor is it necessary to do so. It is
sufficient to say that the Court is a permanent body,
respecting precedent and seeking consistency in its
decisions, and that therefore its view of the Constitution, whether binding on the Executive and the legislature or not, is likely ultimately to prevail as accepted
law.

While it is important to mark out the exclusive field
of jurisdiction of each branch of the government,
Legislative, Executive and Judicial, it should be said
that in the proper working of the government there must
be coöperation of all branches, and without a willingness of each branch to perform its function, there will follow a hopeless obstruction to the progress of the whole
government. Neither branch can compel the other to
affirmative action, and each branch can greatly hinder
the other in the attainment of the object of its activities and the exercise of its discretion. The judicial
branch has sometimes been said to be the most powerful branch of the government because in its decision
of litigated cases it is frequently called upon to mark
the limits of the jurisdiction of the other two branches.
As already noted, by its continuity and the consistency
of its decisions, the Court exercises much greater
power in this regard than the other two branches.
But it has no instruments to enforce its judgments, and

if the Executive fails to remove the obstructions that may be offered to the execution of its decrees and orders, when its authority is defied, then the Court is helpless. It may not directly summon the army or the navy to maintain the supremacy of the law and order. So if the judges of the Court were to refuse to perform the judicial duties imposed by Congress, the object of Congress in much of its legislation might be defeated. And if Congress were to refuse to levy the taxes and make the appropriations which are necessary to pay the salaries of government officials, and to furnish the equipment essential in the performance of their duties, it could paralyze all branches of the government. The life of the government, therefore, depends on the sense of responsibility of each branch in doing the part assigned to it in the carrying on of the business of the people in the government, and ultimately as the last resource, we must look to public opinion as the moving force to induce affirmative action and proper team work. The power over the purse is, however, practically the greatest power, and that Congress exercises without control by either of the other branches. Therefore when fear is expressed of the usurpation by other branches and the thieving of jurisdiction by either, we must keep in mind that the legislative power to withhold appropriations is that which in the history of constitutional government has always been the most powerful agency in the defense of the people's rights.

The true view of the Executive functions is, as I conceive it, that the President can exercise no power which cannot be fairly and reasonably traced to some specific grant of power or justly implied and included within such express grant as proper and necessary to its exercise. Such specific grant must be either in the Federal Constitution or in an act of Congress passed in pursuance thereof. There is no undefined residuum of power which he can exercise because it seems to him to be in the public interest, and there is nothing in the Neagle case and its definition of a law of the United States, or in other precedents, warranting such an inference. The grants of Executive power are necessarily in general terms in order not to embarrass the Executive within the field of action plainly marked for him, but his jurisdiction must be justified and vindicated by affirmative constitutional or statutory provision, or it does not exist. There have not been wanting, however, eminent men in high public office holding a different view and who have insisted upon the necessity for an undefined residuum of Executive power in the public interest. They have not been confined to the present generation. We may learn this from the complaint of a Virginia statesman, Abel P. Upshur, a strict constructionist of the old school, who succeeded Daniel Webster as Secretary of State under President Tyler. He was aroused by Story's commentaries on the Constitution to write a monograph answering and criticizing them, and in the course of this he comments as follows on the Executive power under the Constitution:

The most defective part of the Constitution beyond all question, is that which related to the Executive Department. It is impossible to read that instrument, without being struck with the loose and unguarded terms in which the powers and duties of the President are pointed out. So far as the legislature is concerned, the limitations of the Constitution, are, perhaps, as precise and strict as they could safely have been made; but in regard to the Executive, the Convention appears to have studiously selected such loose and general expressions, as would enable the President, by implication and construction either to neglect his duties or to enlarge his powers. *We have heard it gravely asserted in Congress that whatever power is neither legislative nor judiciary, is of course executive, and, as such, belongs to the President under the Constitution.* How far a majority of that body would have sustained a doctrine so monstrous, and so utterly at war with the whole genius of our government, it is impossible to say, but this, at least, we know, that it met with no rebuke from those who supported the particular act of Executive power, in defense of which it was urged. Be this as it may, it is a reproach to the Constitution that the Executive trust is so ill-defined, as to leave any plausible pretense even to the insane zeal of party devotion, for attributing to the President of the United States the powers of a despot; powers which are wholly unknown in any limited monarchy in the world.

The view that he takes as a result of the loose language defining the Executive powers seems exaggerated. But one must agree with him in his condemnation of the view of the Executive power which he says was advanced in Congress. In recent years there has been put forward a similar view by executive officials and to some extent acted on. Men who are not such strict constructionists of the Constitution as Mr. Upshur may well feel real concern if such views are to receive the general acquiescence. Mr. Garfield, when Secretary of the Interior, under Mr. Roosevelt, in his final report to Congress in reference to the power of the Executive over the public domain, said:

Full power under the Constitution was vested in the Executive Branch of the Government and the extent to which that power may be exercised is governed wholly by the discretion of the Executive unless any specific act has been prohibited either by the Constitution or by legislation.

In pursuance of this principle, Mr. Garfield, under an act for the reclamation of arid land by irrigation, which authorized him to make contracts for irrigation works and incur liability equal to the amount on deposit in the Reclamation Fund, made contracts with associations of settlers by which it was agreed that if these settlers would advance money and work, they might receive certificates from the government engineers of the labor and money furnished by them, and that such certificates might be received in the future in the discharge of their legal obligations to the government for water rent and other things under the statute. It became necessary for the succeeding administration to pass on the validity of these government certificates. They were held by Attorney-General Wickersham to be illegal, on the ground that no authority existed for their issuance. He relied on the Floyd acceptances in 7th Wallace, in which recovery was sought in the Court of Claims on commercial paper in the form of acceptances signed by Mr. Floyd when Secretary of War and delivered to certain contractors. The Court held that they were void because the Secretary of War had no statutory authority to issue them. Mr. Justice Miller, in deciding the case, said :

The answer which at once suggests itself to one familiar with the structure of our government, in which all power is delegated, and is defined by law, constitutional or statutory, is, that to one or both of these sources we must resort in every instance. We have no officers in this government, from the President down to the most subordinate agent, who does not hold office under the law, with prescribed duties and limited authority. And while some of these, as the President, the Legislature, and the Judiciary, exercise powers in some sense left to the more general definitions necessarily incident to fundamental law found in the Constitution, the larger portion of them are the creation of statutory law, with duties and powers prescribed and limited by that law.

In the light of this view of the Supreme Court it is interesting to compare the language of Mr. Roosevelt in his "Notes for a Possible Autobiography" on the subject of "Executive Powers," in which he says:

The most important factor in getting the right spirit in my Administration, next to insistence upon courage, honesty, and a genuine democracy of desire to serve the plain people, was my insistence upon the theory that the executive power was limited only by specific restrictions and prohibitions appearing in the Constitution or imposed by Congress under its constitutional powers. My view was that every Executive officer and above all every Executive officer in high position was a steward of the people bound actively and affirmatively to do all he could for the people and not to content himself with the negative merit of keeping his talents undamaged in a napkin. I declined to adopt this view that what was imperatively necessary for the Nation could not be done by the President, unless he could find some specific authorization to do it. My belief was that it was not only his right but his duty to do anything that the needs of the Nation demanded unless such action was forbidden by the Constitution or by the laws. Under this interpretation of executive power I did and caused to be done many things not previously done by the President and the heads of the departments. I did not usurp power but I did greatly broaden the use of executive power. In other words, I acted for the common well being of all our people whenever and in whatever measure was necessary, unless prevented by direct constitutional or legislative prohibition.

I may add that Mr. Roosevelt, by way of illustrating his meaning as to the differing usefulness of Presidents, divides the Presidents into two classes, and designates them as "Lincoln Presidents" and "Buchanan Presidents." In order more fully to illustrate his division of Presidents on their merits, he places himself in the Lincoln class of Presidents, and me in the Buchanan class. The identification of Mr. Roosevelt with Mr. Lincoln might otherwise have escaped notice, because there are many differences between the two, presumably superficial, which would give the impartial student of history a different impression. It suggests a story which a friend of mine told of his little daughter Mary. As he came walking home after a business day, she ran out from the house to greet him, all aglow with the importance of what she wished to tell him. She said, "Papa, I am the best scholar in the class." The father's heart throbbed with pleasure as he inquired, "Why, Mary, you surprise me. When did the teacher tell you? This afternoon?" "Oh, no," Mary's reply was, "the teacher didn't tell me — I just noticed it myself."

My judgment is that the view of Mr. Garfield and Mr. Roosevelt, ascribing an undefined residuum of power to the President is an unsafe doctrine and that it might lead under emergencies to results of an arbitrary character, doing irremediable injustice to private right. The mainspring of such a view is that the Executive is charged with responsibility for the welfare of all the people in a general way, that he is to play the part of a Universal Providence and set all things right, and that anything that in his judgment will help the people he ought to do, unless he is expressly forbidden not to do it. The wide field of action that this would give to the Executive one can hardly limit. It is enough to say that Mr. Roosevelt has expressly stated how far he thought this principle would justify him in going in respect to the coal famine and the Pennsylvania anthracite strike which he did so much useful work in settling. What was actually done was the result of his activity, his power to influence public opinion and the effect of the prestige of his great office in bringing the parties to the controversy, the mine owners and the strikers, to a legal settlement by arbitration. No one has a higher admiration for the value of what he did there than I have. But if he had failed in this, he says he intended to take action on his theory of the extent of the executive power already stated. I quote from the same book from which his other words are taken. Mr. Roosevelt says:

In my own mind, I was already planning effective action, but it was of a very drastic character, and I did not wish to take it until the failure of all other expedients had rendered it necessary. . . . I had definitely determined that somehow or other, act I would, that somehow or other the coal famine should be broken. To accomplish this end it was necessary that the mines should be run, and if I could get no voluntary agreement between the contending sides, that an arbitration commission should be appointed which would command such public confidence as to enable me without too much difficulty, to enforce its terms on the parties. . . .

*   *   *   *   *   *   *   *

Meanwhile the Governor of Pennsylvania had all the Pennsylvania militia in the anthracite region although without any effect upon the resumption of mining. The method of action upon which I had determined was to get the Governor of Pennsylvania to ask me to keep order. Then I would put in the army under the command of some first rate general. I would instruct this general to keep absolute order, taking any steps whatever that were necessary to prevent interference by the strikers or their sympathizers with men who wanted to work. I would also instruct him to dispossess the operators and run the mines as a receiver until such time as the commission might make its report, and until I as President might issue further orders in view of this report."

Now it is perfectly evident that Mr. Roosevelt thinks he was charged with the duty, not only to suppress disorder in Pennsylvania, but to furnish coal to avoid the coal famine in New York and New England, and therefore he proposed to use the army of the United States to mine the coal which should prevent or relieve the famine. It was his avowed intention to take the coal mines out of the hands of their lawful owners and to mine the coal which belonged to them and sell it in the eastern market, against their objection, without any court proceeding of any kind and without any legal obligation on their part to work the mines at all. It was an advocacy of the higher law and his obligation to execute it which is a little startling in a constitutional republic. It is perfectly evident from his statement that it was not the maintenance of law and order in Pennsylvania and the suppression of insurrection, the *only ground* upon which he could intervene at all, that actuated him in what he proposed to do. He used the expression that he would "get" the Governor of Pennsylvania to call for troops from him, and then having secured a formal authority for the use of the army to suppress disorder, he proposed to use it for the seizure of private property and its appropriation for the benefit of the people of other states. The benevolence of his purpose no one can deny, but no one who looks at it from the standpoint of a government of law could regard it as anything but lawless. I venture to think, however, that Mr. Roosevelt is mistaken in what he thinks he would have done. Mr. Roosevelt in office was properly amenable to the earnest advice of those whom he trusted, and there were men about him who would probably have dissuaded him from such a course.

I am aware that there are many who believe in government ownership of the sources of public comfort in the interest of the community at large; but it is certainly only the extremes of that school that favor the use of the army under the President to seize the needed mines without constitutional amendment or legislative and judicial action and without compensation. Mr. Roosevelt in his subsequent remarks seems to find a justification for his general view of the limitations of Executive power in what Mr. Lincoln did during the Civil War. That Mr. Lincoln with the stress of the greatest civil war in modern times felt called upon to do things, the constitutionality of which was seriously questioned, is undoubtedly true. But Mr. Lincoln always pointed out the source of the authority which in his opinion justified his acts, and there was always a strong ground for maintaining the view which he took. His claim of right to suspend the writ of habeas corpus I venture to think was well founded. Congress subsequently expressly gave him this right and the Supreme Court sustained his exercise of it under the act of Congress. His Emancipation Proclamation was attacked as an unconstitutional exercise of authority, but he defended it as an act of the Commander-in-Chief justified by military necessity to weaken the enemies of the Nation and suppress their rebellion. Certainly the arguments that he and those who supported his action brought to sustain it have great weight. But Mr. Lincoln never claimed that whatever authority in government was not expressly denied to him he could exercise.

In my reading recently I ran across a case which attracted great attention at the time, now more than one hundred years ago. It concerned the action of another President of great popularity, great power, great mental activity, and great and equally genuine sympathy with the people and with popular government — Thomas Jefferson. Mr. Jefferson was a strict constructionist of the Constitution in theory and in practice, but as in the case of all of us, when he had power things looked differently to him and acts were justified in his mind and conscience on the theory that he was doing good and working for the public welfare. But in his wide view of what he himself as President could do to preserve the public welfare, he did something that troubled him, even after he left the Presidency.

The owner of a large tract of land reaching to the Mississippi River, just outside of New Orleans, and a part of its suburbs, claimed title to an alluvial extension of that land deposited by the river, as lawful accretion to his property. Such an accretion was known in French legal nomenclature as a " Batture." The owner sought by suit in the Territorial Court to exclude from the Batture people of the city who took sand therefrom. The Territorial Court sustained the title of the riparian owner to the Batture. In this litigation Edward Livingston, who had gone from New York to New Orleans, just after the acquisition of the Territory, appeared as counsel for the owner and as part of his compensation received some of the land. He attempted to improve it, to protect it against the wearing of the river and to build a canal through it. The territorial governor was Claiborn, and the people of the town who had been shut out by the action of the local court appealed to him. He submitted the matter to Mr. Jefferson, who consulted his Attorney-General, Mr. Rodney, and thereupon issued a warrant directing the United States Marshal to take possession of the land in question and hold it for the benefit of the people of New Orleans, under a Statute of Congress authorizing the President to exclude squatters from the public domain. The local court issued an injunction against the marshal's complying with this order of the President. The marshal refused to obey the injunction, and using Federal troops opened the land to the use of the people of the city, who continued to take sand. This exposed the land to the danger which it was being improved to prevent. The river rose and swept away the works. Livingston lost a very large sum of money by reason of this invasion. He went to Washington twice, to be heard, and was refused an opportunity to argue the case, or to know the grounds upon which action of the President had been taken, or to see the opinion of the Attorney-General upon which it was based. He petitioned Congress for relief without avail. Finally he brought suit against Jefferson personally for trespass in the Federal Court of Virginia. The suit was dismissed by Chief Justice Marshall of the Federal Court on the ground that the court in Virginia had no jurisdiction of a trespass committed on land in Louisiana.

Thereafter Mr. Jefferson published a defense of his action which brought out an answer from Livingston, which was so convincing on the issues made by Mr. Jefferson and was so replete with wit and humor and satire that even the British Encyclopedia describes it as crushing. In the course of this answer Livingston used some language that it seems to me would have been properly applicable to the proceeding which Mr. Roosevelt proposed to take, and which he frankly calls drastic. Mr. Roosevelt says there would doubtless have been an outcry against his proceeding. It would have been denounced as a usurpation; but he thinks that the good he would have done would have rallied to his support the great body of the people in whose interest he would have acted and thus his plan would have vindicated itself. Mr. Livingston opened his answer to Jefferson as follows:

When a public functionary abuses his power by an act which bears on the community, his conduct excites attention, provokes popular resentment, and seldom fails to receive the punishment it merits. Should an individual be chosen for the victim, little sympathy is created for his sufferings, if the interest of all is supposed to be promoted by the ruin of one. The gloss of zeal for the public is therefore always spread over acts of oppression, and as a brilliant exertion of energy in their favor, which, when viewed in its true light, would be found a fatal blow to their rights.

In no government is this effect so easily produced as in a free republic; party spirit, inseparable from its existence, there aids the illusion, and a popular leader is allowed in many instances impunity, and sometimes rewarded with applause for acts that would make a tyrant tremble on his throne. This evil must exist in a degree — it is founded in the natural course of human passions; but in a wise and enlightened nation it will be restrained; and the consciousness that it must exist will make such a people more watchful to prevent its abuse. These reflections occur to one, whose property, without trial or any of the forms of law, has been violently seized by the first magistrate of the Union, — who has hitherto vainly solicited an inquiry into his title, — who has seen the conduct of his oppressor excused or applauded, — and who, in the book he is now about to examine, finds an attempt openly to justify that conduct upon principles as dangerous as the act was illegal and unjust.

Mr. Livingston ended his answer to Mr. Jefferson as follows :

My future conduct will depend much on that of my adversary. I shall continue to reply to every argument that may be addressed to the public on this subject. Knowing that my cause is good, I do not despair, even with humble pretensions, to make its justice appear. For this purpose, I have always courted investigation: I should have preferred it in a court of justice, but do not decline it before the public.

Though some may condemn me only on hearing the name of my opponent, there are many, very many, in the nation who have independence enough to judge for themselves, and the ability to decide with correctness; to such I submit the merits of a controversy which has been rendered interesting as well from the constitutional as the legal questions it involves, and on which Mr. Jefferson has, by his management of it, staked his legal, his political, and almost his moral reputation. That he should not have understood the nature of my title and the different foreign codes on which it depends, is no reproach; that he should have acted at all without this knowledge must surprise, that he should have acted forcibly, must astonish us; but that he should persevere in the same pretence of understanding the law of France better than gentlemen bred to it from their childhood, and who, engaged in the same side of the controversy with himself, have abandoned the ground he has taken — that he should obstinately justify an invasion of private property, in a manner that puts it in the power of a President with impunity to commit acts of oppression at which a King would tremble — that he should do all this, and still talk of conscious rectitude, must amaze all those who look only to the reputation he has enjoyed, and who do not consider the inconsistency of human nature, and the deplorable effects of an inordinate passion for popularity.

The life of Edward Livingston is one of the most romantic and checkered that I know. He was a brother of Chancellor Livingston, and a son of an earlier Judge Livingston. He was born in the Colony of New York, and was given a thorough education in languages and in both the common and the civil law. He was a gifted speaker and had a style both pleasant and trenchant, which he illuminated with wit, humor and satire and with the most graceful literary references. He was a very earnest Republican and a follower of Jefferson. He was elected to Congress as a Republican in the days of the first Adams, and introduced the resolutions, already noted, denouncing Adams as a usurper of individual right in granting the extradition of the British murderer who was arrested in South Carolina. These resolutions were the occasion for the wonderful argument of John Marshall, also a member of Congress, to which I have referred. After Mr. Livingston had served in Congress for two terms, he was appointed by Mr. Jefferson to be United States District Attorney for New York. He was also at the same time (for they allowed plurality of offices in those days), appointed to be Mayor of New York by Governor Clinton. Mr. Livingston was a free liver and most hospitable. The yellow fever came to New York. As Mayor, Mr. Livingston was active in dealing with the epidemic and endeared himself to the people by his efforts to save them.   During the epidemic, an agent of the government visited New York, examined Mr. Livingston's accounts and found that in his collections for the government he was short a large sum.   It at first was thought to be one hundred thousand dollars, but was subsequently found to be not more than forty thousand.   It turned out that a good deal of this was due to the dishonesty of a subordinate, but Livingston could not relieve himself entirely from the charge of defalcation which was probably due to his lack of care in his accounts.   When the matter was brought to his attention, he resigned both offices, turned all his property over to the government, and left for New Orleans, a territory which in the year before, in 1803, had been taken over by the United States under a treaty negotiated by his brother, Chancellor Robert Livingston.   By his defalcation he passed out of the good graces of Mr. Jefferson, and Mr. Jefferson's attitude in respect to the litigation in which Mr. Livingston took part is possibly explained by his irritation at the disgrace which he felt that Livingston had put upon his administration.   Though ruined by the action of Mr. Jefferson in respect to the Batture, Mr. Livingston continued the practice of the law and paid the Government in full.   He was in New Orleans at the time of the famous battle fought there by Old Hickory.   General Jackson came to know Mr. Livingston and to value him highly, and used him for legal advice before and after the battle.   Mr. Livingston appeared for General Jackson in responding to a summons issued by Judge Hall for contempt on the part of the General in ignoring a writ of *habeas corpus* which he had issued, and in otherwise treating the Judge contemptuously. After the battle, General Jackson recognized the jurisdiction of the court, and submitted to its authority, upon Mr. Livingston's advice. The friendship made with General Jackson, Mr. Livingston continued to enjoy during his life. He subsequently became a member of Congress from Louisiana, a United States Senator from the state, and was finally appointed Secretary of State under General Jackson. Mr. Livingston wrote a code of procedure for the Territory of Louisiana to reconcile the civil law practice to the anomalies which the adoption of the state into a Union with so many common law jurisdictions presented. This code was adopted. The great reputation which Mr. Livingston obtained, however, was from a criminal code which he wrote for the state of Louisiana, but which that state did not adopt. In its humanity and its provisions for prison reform, it was fifty years ahead of his time.

I venture to say that no American jurist among the jurists of continental Europe made a deeper impression than did Mr. Livingston by his Criminal Code. It is of the utmost interest to note the fact that after he had published his code and had received from it the highest commendations from Chief Justice Marshall, Chancellor Kent and Mr. Justice Story, and all the great jurists of the country, Mr. Jefferson wrote him a letter congratulating him upon it and assuring him of his respect and friendship. After Mr. Jefferson's death, Mr. Livingston was arguing a case in the Supreme Court of the United States when the other side quoted from his answer to Jefferson as to the Batture. In the course of his argument he referred to the answer and said that it was written under a sense of having a great wrong done him by Mr. Jefferson, and that he had not changed his view since writing it. But he said he thought he owed it to the memory of Mr. Jefferson to say that in after years Mr. Jefferson renewed his friendly relations with him, and showed by his conduct the greatness which a French writer recognizes in a man who having done an injury to another is able to forgive that other.

Recurring now to the plan of Mr. Roosevelt as to the coal mines of Pennsylvania, I think that if we substitute for the individual Livingston, in the Batture controversy, the anthracite mine owners, the language of Mr. Livingston which I have quoted would be germane in such a discussion. I would not dwell upon this subject were it not of great importance with reference to the course urged upon President Wilson when he had sent Federal troops for the maintenance of order in Colorado. He was advised to use the troops to close the mines which were then running and producing a substantial part of their normal product. The closing of mines might have been a sop to those who threatened violence in case the troops were withdrawn and so mitigate lawlessness for a time. But was it a proper method of maintaining order to deprive men of the right of property that it was the very object of the constitutional provision for Federal intervention to protect? No one claimed the operation of the mines was unlawful. It was only said that their continued operation after the withdrawal of the Federal troops would lead to disturbance. By whom? By the strikers. Was this not a proposition to compel an owner of property to cease its lawful use because his former employees would otherwise attempt unlawfully and violently to prevent such use?

I have now concluded a review of the Executive power, and hope that I have shown that it is limited, so far as it is possible to limit such a power consistent with that discretion and promptness of action that are essential to preserve the interests of the public in times of emergency, or legislative neglect or inaction.

There is little danger to the public weal from the tyranny or reckless character of a President who is not sustained by the people. The absence of popular support will certainly in the course of two years withdraw from him the sympathetic action of at least one House of Congress, and by the control that that House has over appropriations, the Executive arm can be paralyzed, unless he resorts to a coup d'état, which means impeachment, conviction and deposition. The only danger in the action of the Executive under the present limitations and lack of limitation of his powers is when his popularity is such that he can be sure of the support of the electorate and therefore of Congress, and when the majority in the legislative halls respond with alacrity and sycophancy to his will. This condition cannot probably be long continued. We have had Presidents who felt the public pulse with accuracy, who played their parts upon the political stage with histrionic genius and commanded the people almost as if they were an army and the President their Commander-in-Chief. Yet in all these cases, the good sense of the people has ultimately prevailed and no danger has been done to our political structure and the reign of law has continued. In such times when the Executive power seems to be all prevailing, there have always been men in this free and intelligent people of ours, who apparently courting political humiliation and disaster have registered protest against this undue Executive domination and this use of the Executive power and popular support to perpetuate itself.

The cry of Executive domination is often entirely unjustified, as when the President's commanding influence only grows out of a proper cohesion of a party and its recognition of the necessity for political leadership; but the fact that Executive domination is regarded as a useful ground for attack upon a successful administration, even when there is no ground for it, is itself proof of the dependence we may properly place upon the sanity and clear perceptions of the people in avoiding its baneful effects when there is real danger.   Even if a vicious precedent is set by the Executive, and injustice done, it does not have the same bad effect that an improper precedent of a court may have, for one President does not consider himself bound by the policies or constitutional views of his predecessors.

The Constitution does give the President wide discretion and great power, and it ought to do so.   It calls from him activity and energy to see that within his proper sphere he does what his great responsibilities and opportunities require.   He is no figurehead, and it is entirely proper that an energetic and active clear-sighted people, who, when they have work to do, wish it done well, should be willing to rely upon their judgment in selecting their Chief Agent, and having selected him, should entrust to him all the power needed to carry out their governmental purpose, great as it may be.

INDEX

Act of War, What constitutes an, 95–96

Adams, President, did not veto bills on merits, 16; opposed by Livingston, 86; warrant by, upheld by Court, 87; appointed "Midnight Judges," 42. See Jay's Treaty

Amnesty, granted by the President, 119; effect of, 119–120

Appointment Power, to whom applies, 55–56; how exercised, 61–64; dangers of, 68; is a tax upon the President, 67–71; is not good for the Court, 70; in what officers advantageous, 72; of the President, is limited by Congress, 125; may be exercised free of encroachment, 126–128

Appropriation Bills, may include irrelevant legislation of a hostile Congress, 25–27; may arise from a treaty obligation, 115. See Budget

Appropriation Act, Construction of, and procedure, 81

Arthur, President, vetoed bill encroaching upon appointment power, 126

Bank of the United States, Renewal of charter of the, vetoed, 136. See Veto

Bills, must be signed by the President or returned, 23–24; vetoed, 25–27; passed over veto, 25. See Veto

Blaine, Mr., Secretary of State, 118

Branches of Government, Origin and powers of the, 1–2

"Buchanan Presidents," 144

Budget, Lack of, in the United States, a mistake, 4–5; English

system, 5–7; appearance in proposed New York constitution shows progress, 7–8, 28; would check extravagance, 8, 28; recommended by a Commission, but not popular with Congress, 64–65

Buenos Aires, Violation of sealing laws of, decided by President as a political issue, 117–118

Cabinet, The term does not occur in the Constitution, but in statutes and judicial opinions, 29; origin and purpose of, 30; compared with that of England, 30–31; officers should have more influence and access to Congress, 31–32; meetings are informal, 33; is better than a directory, 35–37; dissension in Washington's, 36; in Lincoln's, 35, 37

Canal Zone, Government of, 93–94; boundaries of, 111–112

China, Boxer uprising in, 114

Chinese, Bill for exclusion of, vetoed, 17; entitled to immigrate by treaty, excluded by Congress, 109

Circuit Court Acts, 43

Civil Service, Number of employees under the, 58; effect of, 59; growth of, 58–59; preserves the continuity of government, 84; relation of President to, 84–85

Classified Service, Unpopular with Congress, 65; not without dangers, 66

Cleveland, President, Vetoes by, were frequent, 17; upheld as Commander-in-Chief of the Army, 97

Commander-in-Chief of the Army and Navy, 94–99, 114, 128–129

159

in England under, 6; compared
with power of the President, 9;
is less rigid in division into
branches, 10; history of veto
power under, 15; cabinet under,
30–31
Party, Political, helps the President,
12; may block the President and
increase vetoes, 17; patronage
favored by Congress, 65, 67; by
reformers, 67–68
Patents, 80
Patronage, of Congress cannot be
broken up, 61–62, 65–68; wrong in
the Federal Courts, 69–70
Pension Bills, vetoed when Congress
is hostile to the President, 17, 80
Philippine Act, Interpretation of,
by the Supreme Court, a joke on
the framers, 101
Philippines, The, governed by the
President as Commander-in-Chief
of the Army and Navy, 98–102;
appropriation bill for, 134
Platt Amendment, 87–88
Pocket Veto, 23
Political Parties. See Party
Polk, President, 95
Porto Rico, 98–99
Postmasters, appointed by the President, 60–61
Postmaster-General, The, may make
treaties, 135
President, Favors by the, are few,
49; is not forbidden to leave the
country, 50; is protected by the
Secret Service, 51; stands for
the government to the people, 52;
is often unjustly criticized for
policy and acts, 52–53; tax on,
of appointments to office, 67–74;
how a sense of humor in, lightens
the routine, 73–75; centering of
responsibility in, is wise, 76;
oath of, 78; has little effect upon
the machinery of government,
84–85; not obliged to perform
all acts at the seat of government,
130; is regarded as beyond the
compulsory process of the Court,
132–133; may withdraw lands
open for settlement, 136. See

Appointment, Cuban Treaty, Executive Power, Pardon, Patronage,
Treaties, Veto
——, Commander-in-Chief of the
Army and Navy, 94–99; 114,
128–129
——, The Duties of, should include framing a budget, 8; to
preserve the Constitution, 19;
to execute the laws, 78; which
includes protecting life of judges,
88–92, protecting citizens against
foreign aggression, 92, protecting
a person arrested, 92–93
——, The Judicial Powers of, in-
terpretations under, are final, 79;
no general, 83
——, The Limitations on, by the
Court, 47–48. See Supreme Court,
Congress
——, The Office of, is not one of
record, 34
——, The Political Powers of,
enable him to recognize a foreign
government, 96; a state governor,
98; foreign ambassadors, 113;
to regulate foreign relations, appoint ambassadors, 104–105; to
make treaties, 105–106; to frame
a foreign policy through the Secretary of State, 113; to annul a
treaty, 115–116; to decide viola-
tions of sealing laws of a foreign
jurisdiction, 118
——, The Powers of, are hard to
define, 2–3; centralization of, 3;
compared with rulers of Europe,
9; are limited by Congress, 125;
some created by custom, 135–136
——, Relations of, with Congress, should be closer, 4–5;
often produce friction and vetoes,
12–14; no initiative, but recommendations for legislation lies
in the President, 11–14; should
not allow a bill to become law
without his signature, 24; should
allow initiative with the President, 31; may seek advice and
consent of the Senate in person,
37–39; or by written message,
40; oral addresses are preferable,

Upshur, Mr. Abel P., believed Executive power too broad, 140–141

Van Buren, President, Expenditures by, criticized by hostile Congress, 18

Veto, The, Debated in the Continental Congress, 3–4; is a legislative act, 14; how power of, is exercised, 14; must apply to the whole of a bill, 14, 25, 27; origin of, 15; does not depend on constitutionality but on approval, 15–16; frequency of, in President Johnson's administration and others, 17; brings well-worn criticisms upon the President, 18; should be exercised when bill seems unconstitutional, 19; has not been exercised by King of England for 200 years, 18–19; gives broader legislative function than has the Supreme Court, 19–21; governors fail to exercise, when bill is popular, 22; must be exercised within ten days, 24;

of part of a bill might cure the "rider" evil, 27; is the only legislative function of the President, 29. *See* Congress

War, is declared by Congress, 95–96; in effect may be declared by the President, 95; act of, distinguished from police duty, 95–96; what constitutes an act of, 96

Warner, Barnes & Co., suit of, against the United States, 99–102

Washington, President, and the Continental Congress, 3; vetoes by, were not on the merits, 16; Cabinet of, 35–37; personal visits of, to the Senate, 37–39; character of, 39; controversy with Congress over Jay's Treaty, 130

Webb Bill, The, vetoed by President Taft, 21

White House, The, is a very appropriate residence, 49–50

White, Mr. Justice, 102–103

Wilson, President, revives the custom of oral address to Congress, 40